The SCHEME Programming Language

R. Kent Dybvig

Indiana University
Bloomington, Indiana

Prentice-Hall, Inc. Englewood Cliffs, New Jersey 07632

Library of Congress Catalog Card Number: 86-63489.

Editorial/production supervision: Barbara Marttine Webber
Cover design: Lundgren Graphics, Ltd.
Manufacturing buyer: S. Gordon Osbourne

The publisher offers discounts on this book when ordered
in bulk quantities. For more information, write:

> Special Sales/College Marketing
> Prentice-Hall, Inc.
> College Technical and Reference Division
> Englewood Cliffs, NJ 07632

ISBN   0-13-791864-X   025

Prentice-Hall International (UK) Limited, *London*
Prentice-Hall of Australia Pty. Limited, *Sydney*
Prentice-Hall Canada Inc., *Toronto*
Prentice-Hall Hispanoamericana, S.A., *Mexico*
Prentice-Hall of India Private Limited, *New Delhi*
Prentice-Hall of Japan, Inc., *Tokyo*
Prentice-Hall of Southeast Asia Pte. Ltd., *Singapore*
Editora Prentice-Hall do Brasil, Ltda., *Rio de Janeiro*

Contents

Foreword

For reasons that we don't fully understand, Lisp and its recent offspring, Scheme, seem to delight the senses. Scheme programmers are not just interested in the solution to a problem but pride themselves on looking for the most elegant solution, the one whose beauty is self-evident.

A computer language should provide an environment in which the programmer can creatively produce good computational models or paradigms for the problems at hand. The programmer's ability to construct paradigms should not be restricted. I call the ease of constructing paradigms the language's "paradigmicity." Languages with low paradigmicity are *boring*. Programmers should not be straitjacketed. The creativity of humans is too diverse, our computing needs too varied, and our love of aesthetics too great to be hobbled by languages with low paradigmicity.

Does high paradigmicity imply complexity? Hardly. Arithmetic has high paradigmicity. With it we've traveled to the moon and managed to do the accounting necessary to run the world's businesses. Was the discovery of calculus impeded by arithmetic's simplicity? Or is it perhaps the other way around—that high paradigmicity must coexist with simplicity? I believe the latter to be the case.

How do we create languages with high paradigmicity? We introduce a few fundamental concepts, a few ways of combining these concepts, and in doing so we take advantage of years of experience in solving problems.

No popular programming language in existence today has more paradigmicity than Scheme. Its fundamental concepts are procedures, continuations, engines, conditionals, and assignment-statements. Everything is closed under composition and recursion, and there is provision for both syntactic and semantic extension.

If you are learning Scheme be warned that the learning curve is rather steep. It is in the very nature of a high paradigmicity language that it requires mental effort to fully comprehend all of its subtleties and power. We don't do number theory until we learn about numbers and arithmetic. Each person will see different uses for Scheme in much the same way as people see different uses for arithmetic. The skill of a Scheme programmer varies from that of other Scheme programmers just as with people who use arithmetic. The more experience and practice one gets with using its fundamental concepts, the quicker new paradigms emerge.

At last there is a book which covers the whole language. Kent Dybvig has done an excellent job of laying out all the details while at the same time giving the reader challenging things to reflect upon at every turn. Mastery of the subject is at hand.

Daniel P. Friedman

Preface

Scheme was introduced in 1975 by Gerald J. Sussman and Guy L. Steele, Jr. [19,17], as the first dialect of Lisp to fully support static scoping, first-class procedures, and continuations. In its earliest form it was a very small language intended primarily for research and teaching, supporting only a handful of predefined syntactic forms and procedures. Although modern implementations of Scheme support more syntactic forms and procedures, Scheme is still relatively small and derives most of its power from a small set of concepts.

This book is intended to provide an introduction to the Scheme language but not an introduction to programming in general. The reader is expected to have had some experience with Scheme or another programming language and to be familiar with terms commonly associated with computers and programming languages. The author highly recommends that readers unfamiliar with Scheme or Lisp first read *The Little LISPer* [4] to become familiar with the concepts of list processing and recursion.

This book is not a language definition or standard document for Scheme. There is a separate report, the "Revised[3] Report on the Algorithmic Language Scheme" [15] that defines a standard subset of Scheme intended to be supported by all Scheme implementations. The Revised[3] Report makes it possible to write programs that may be run on any version of Scheme supporting the standard subset and should be consulted when portability is required. This book does include all of the features required to support the standard subset, and nearly all of the non-required features mentioned in the report as having a standard meaning. The Summary of Forms appearing near the end of this book identifies which syntactic forms and procedures are part of the standard subset.

A large number of small to medium-sized examples are spread throughout the text, and one entire chapter is dedicated to the presentation of a set of longer examples. Many of the examples show how a predefined Scheme syntactic form or procedure might be implemented. Nearly all Scheme systems are interactive, and all of the examples can be entered directly from the keyboard into an interactive Scheme session.

All of the features described in this book are supported by the *Chez* Scheme implementation of Scheme. Some of the examples depend upon

x The SCHEME Programming Language

features peculiar to *Chez* Scheme, but many can be run with little or no modification in a Scheme system that supports the standard subset.

This book is organized into nine chapters. Chapter 1 describes the properties and features of Scheme that make it a useful and enjoyable language to use. Because it presumes more knowledge of programming languages than some readers may have, it may be best in some cases to delay reading Chapter 1 until after having completed Chapter 2. Chapter 1 also describes Scheme's notational conventions and the typographical conventions employed in this book.

Chapter 2 is an introduction to Scheme programming for the novice Scheme programmer, leading the reader through a series of examples, beginning with the simplest Scheme expressions and working toward progressively more difficult ones. Each section of Chapter 2 introduces a small set of related features, and at the end of each section is a set of exercises for further practice. The reader will learn the most from Chapter 2 by sitting at the keyboard and typing in the examples and trying the exercises.

Chapters 3 through 8 make up the reference portion of the text. They present each of Scheme's procedures and syntactic forms in turn, grouping them into short sections of related procedures and forms. Chapter 3 describes operations for creating and assigning identifier bindings (including procedure definition); Chapter 4, program control operations; Chapter 5, operations on the various object types (including lists, numbers, and strings); Chapter 6, input and output operations; Chapter 7, system operations (such as loading or compiling files or tracing procedures); and Chapter 8, syntactic extension and structure definition.

Because the reference portion is separated into groups of related features, most readers will find it profitable to read through most of the material to become familiar with each feature and how it relates to other similar features. However, Chapter 5 is lengthy, describing a great number of useful operations on Scheme objects. It should be skimmed and later referred to as needed. Refer to the Summary of Forms or to the Index at the back of the book to find where a particular syntactic form or procedure is described.

Finally, Chapter 9 is a collection of complete example programs or packages, each with a short overview, some examples of its use, the implementation with brief explanation, and a set of exercises for further work. Each of these programs demonstrates a particular set of features, and together they provide a picture of the author's style of programming in Scheme.

I would like to express my gratitude to the many people who have assisted me in the preparation of this book. First among them is Bruce Smith, who helped with many aspects of the book, including writing the early drafts of Chapter 2 and reviewing the remainder of the text. Several others have contributed by providing me with many comments and assistance along the way, especially Eugene Kohlbecker, Matthias Felleisen, Dan Friedman, Bruce Duba, Phil Dybvig, and Guy Steele. Others who have reviewed portions of the text or contributed their ideas include Bob Hieb, Chris Haynes, Dave Plaisted, Joan Curry, and Frank Silbermann. My gratitude also goes to John Wait and others at Prentice-Hall for their guidance in the writing and production of this book. Numerous Indiana University Computer Science students have used *Chez* Scheme for three semesters in a variety of sophomore-level through graduate-level courses. Many have offered comments or criticisms which have led to several improvements in both the system and the book. Many associations with various people and groups have aided or influenced my study of Scheme and Computer Science and other things, including Rob Vollum, Arol Ambler, and others at Data General in Research Triangle Park, Gyula Magó, Don Stanat and others at The University of North Carolina at Chapel Hill, George Cohn, Mr. Jerry Neff, and especially my parents, Roger S. Dybvig and Elizabeth H. Dybvig and the rest of my family. I wish to express special thanks to Fred, who stayed up with me many long nights listening to my ramblings on the finer points of Scheme. Finally, I wish to thank my wife, Susan Dybvig, whose assistance, hard work, good ideas, and understanding were all of great value throughout the writing of this book.

R. Kent Dybvig
Bloomington, Indiana

Chapter 1: Introduction

Scheme is a general-purpose computer programming language. It is a high-level language, supporting operations on structured data such as strings, lists and vectors, as well as operations on more traditional data such as numbers and characters. Scheme is a fairly simple language to learn, since it is based on a handful of syntactic forms and semantic concepts, and since its interactive nature encourages experimentation. However, Scheme is a challenging language to understand fully; the use of its full potential requires careful study and practice.

While Scheme is often identified with artificial intelligence applications, its rich set of object (data) types and flexible control structures make it a truly versatile language. Scheme has been employed to write full-screen editors, optimizing compilers, operating systems, graphics packages, and numerical applications programs.

Scheme supports operations on many types of objects, including numbers, characters, strings, symbols, and lists or vectors of objects. Objects are allocated in a heap and automatically deallocated when they are no longer needed, freeing the programmer from explicit storage management. A full set of numeric data types, including complex, real, and arbitrary-precision rational numbers, allows Scheme to support many numerical applications typically coded in lower-level languages.

At the heart of the Scheme language is a small core of syntactic forms from which all other forms are built. These core forms, a set of extended syntactic forms derived from them, and a library of primitive procedures make up the full Scheme language. An interpreter or compiler for Scheme can be quite small, and potentially fast and highly reliable. The extended syntactic forms and many primitive procedures are defined in Scheme itself, simplifying the implementation and increasing reliability.

Since Scheme supports automatic storage management, high-level input and output facilities, a library of procedures operating on a rich set of object types, and an interactive programming system, it is not surprising that its demands for computer memory are high compared with those some other languages. Still, Scheme is small enough that it has been successfully implemented on 16- and 32-bit microprocessors with 512 kilobytes or 1 megabyte of memory. Reasonable subsets have even run on 8-bit microcomputers with only 64 kilobytes of memory.

Although some early Scheme systems were inefficient and slow, many newer Scheme implementations are fast, with some programs running as fast as or faster than equivalent programs written in relatively low-level languages. This is due, in part, to recent innovations in the implementation of Scheme. It is also due to the ability of a Scheme compiler to focus on the small set of core forms. The relative inefficiency that remains results from run-time checks that help the programmer to detect and correct various common programming errors.

Scheme programs are highly portable across implementations of the same Scheme dialect on different machines, because machine dependencies are completely hidden from the programmer. Also, because of a recent effort by a group of Scheme designers, it is now possible to use a standard subset of Scheme to write programs that are portable across different Scheme dialects. This subset is described in the "Revised[3] Report on the Algorithmic Language Scheme" [15]. The examples in this book were written and tested using *Chez* Scheme, and some use features not supported by all Scheme implementations. However, many of the examples will run in any Scheme system that supports the standard subset.

Scheme handles data values (numbers, strings, symbols, lists, *etc.*) quite differently from most languages. Data values, or *objects*, are dynamically allocated in a heap where they are retained until no longer needed, then automatically deallocated. Objects are *first-class* data values; because they are heap-allocated and retained indefinitely, they may be passed freely as arguments to procedures, returned as values from procedures, and combined to form new objects. This is in contrast with most other languages where composite data values such as arrays are either statically allocated and never deallocated, or allocated on entry to a block of code and always deallocated on exit from the block.

Scheme programs are represented syntactically (and internally, prior to compilation and execution) as lists, symbols, and other objects supported by Scheme. For example, identifiers are represented by symbols, and most other syntactic forms by lists. This representation is the basis of the syntactic extension facilities provided by most Scheme systems for the definition of new syntactic forms in terms of existing syntactic forms and procedures. It also facilitates the implementation of interpreters, compilers, and other program transformation tools for Scheme directly in Scheme, as well as program transformation tools for other languages in Scheme.

Scheme identifiers are *statically scoped*. Statically scoped identifiers may be referenced only within a particular *block* of code apparent in the structure of the program. A reference to a identifier of the same name outside this block refers to a different identifier; if no such identifier exists, then the reference is invalid. Blocks may be nested, and it is possible for a identifier in one block to shadow a identifier of the same name in a surrounding block. Block structure and static scoping help create programs that are modular, easy to read, easy to maintain, and reliable. Efficient code for static scoping is possible because a compiler can determine easily the scope of all identifiers and the target of each identifier reference and assignment. This does not mean the compiler can determine the value of any identifier, since the actual binding of identifiers to values does not occur until the program executes.

In most languages, a procedure definition is simply the association of a name with a block of code. Certain identifiers local to the block are the parameters of the procedure. In some languages, a procedure definition may appear within another block or procedure so long as the procedure is invoked only during execution of the enclosing block. In Scheme, a procedure definition may appear within another block or procedure, and the procedure may be invoked at any time thereafter, even if the enclosing block has completed its execution. Scheme ensures that all identifier references and assignments within the procedure obey the static scoping rules, *i.e.*, they occur within the scope of the block enclosing the procedure definition. Scheme procedures are not always named. Instead, procedures are first-class data objects similar to strings or numbers; identifiers are bound to procedures in the same way they are bound to other objects. To support the static scoping, a procedure carries the static context along with its code.

As with procedures in most other languages, Scheme procedures may be recursive. That is, any procedure may invoke itself directly or indirectly. Many algorithms are most elegantly or efficiently specified recursively. A special case of recursion, called tail recursion, is used to implement loops. A *tail call* occurs when one procedure returns the result of invoking another procedure directly; *tail recursion* occurs when a procedure recursively tail calls itself, directly or indirectly. Scheme implementations are required to implement tail calls as jumps (gotos), so the storage overhead normally associated with recursion is avoided and tail recursion executes as a loop. As a result, a programmer need only master simple procedure calls and recursion, and need not be burdened with the usual assortment of looping constructs.

Scheme supports the definition of arbitrary control structures with *continuations*. A continuation is a procedure that embodies the state of a program at a given point. When a continuation is invoked, the program immediately continues from that point. A continuation may be created at any time during the execution of a program. As with other procedures, a continuation is a first class object and may be invoked at any time after its creation. Continuations allow the implementation of complex control mechanisms including explicit backtracking and coroutines.

Most dialects of Scheme allow programmers to define extended syntactic forms in terms of existing syntactic forms and procedures. Syntactic extensions are useful for defining new language constructs, for emulating language constructs found in other languages, or even for emulating entire languages in Scheme. Most large programs are built from a mix of syntactic extensions and procedure definitions.

Some dialects of Scheme support multitasking with *engines*. Engines are procedures that execute for a specified time before returning either an answer, if the time was sufficient, or a new engine, if the time was not sufficient. Engines can be used to implement operating system kernels or to simulate multiprocessor systems.

Scheme evolved from the Lisp language and is considered to be a dialect of Lisp. Scheme inherited from Lisp the treatment of values as first-class objects, several important data types, including symbols and lists, and the representation of programs as objects, among other things. Static scoping and block structure are features taken from Algol 60 [13]. Scheme was the first Lisp dialect to adopt static scoping and block structure, the notion of first-class procedures, treatment of tail calls as jumps, and continuations.

Common Lisp [18], whose development was influenced by Scheme (as was Scheme's development subsequently influenced by Common Lisp), adopted static scoping and first-class procedures. However, Common Lisp's evaluation rules for procedures are different from the evaluation rules for other objects, and it maintains a separate namespace for procedure identifiers, thereby discouraging the use of procedures as first-class objects. Common Lisp does not support continuations or optimized tail calls, but it does support a number of features not found in Scheme, most of which are designed to facilitate the development of large program systems. While the two dialects Scheme and Common Lisp are similar, the differences tend to make Scheme more suitable for system design, research, and teaching and tend to make Common Lisp more suitable for the development of large-scale production systems.

same implementation, or even the same across two uses of the procedure or syntactic form.

This book sometimes says "it is an error" or "an error will be signaled" when describing a circumstance in violation of the rules of Scheme. When we say something is an error, we mean that it is not valid in Scheme and that the action of the system in such a case is not specified. When we say something will cause an error to be signaled, we mean that the error handler is invoked with a message describing the error.

The typographic conventions used in this book are straightforward. All Scheme objects are printed in a `typewriter` font, just as if they were typed at the keyboard. This includes syntactic keywords, procedure identifiers, constant objects, Scheme expressions, and example programs. An *italic* font is used to set off syntax variables in the description of syntactic forms and arguments in the description of procedures. Italics are also used to set off a technical term the first time it appears. In general, syntax keywords and procedure names written in a typewriter font are never capitalized (even when the word begins a sentence). The same is true for syntax variables written in an italic font.

In the description of syntactic forms or procedures, a pattern shows the syntactic form or the application of the procedure. The syntax keyword or procedure name is given in a typewriter font, as are parentheses and brackets. The remaining pieces of the syntax or arguments are shown in italics, using a name that implies the type of expression or argument expected by the syntactic form or procedure. Ellipses are used to specify zero or more occurrences of a subexpression or argument. For example, (or *exp* ...) describes the or syntactic form, which expects zero or more expressions, and (set-car! *pair* *obj*) describes the set-car! procedure, which expects two arguments, a pair and an object.

```
(cdr '(a b c)))   ⇒  (a b c)
```

As you can see, Scheme expressions may span more than one line. The Scheme system knows when it has an entire expression by matching double quotes and parentheses.

Next, let's try defining a procedure.

```
(define square
   (lambda (n)
      (* n n)))
```

The procedure square computes the square n^2 of any number n. We say more about the expressions that make up this procedure later in this chapter. For now it suffices to say that define establishes identifier values, lambda creates procedures, and * names the multiplication procedure. Note the form of these expressions. All Scheme expressions are written in prefix notation, *i.e.*, the operator precedes the arguments. As you can see, this is true even for simple arithmetic operations such as *.

Try using square.

```
(square 5)      ⇒  25
(square -200)   ⇒  40000
(square 1/2)    ⇒  1/4
```

Even though the next definition is short, you might wish to try using a text editor to enter it into a file. Call the file "reciprocal.ss".

```
(define reciprocal
   (lambda (n)
      (if (= n 0)
          "oops!"
          (/ 1 n))))
```

This procedure, reciprocal, computes the quantity $1/n$ for any number $n \neq 0$. For $n = 0$, reciprocal returns the string "oops!". Return to Scheme and try loading your file with the procedure load.

```
(load "reciprocal.ss")
```

Finally, try using the procedure we have just defined.

```
(reciprocal 10)     ⇒  1/10
(reciprocal 1/10)   ⇒  10
(reciprocal 0)      ⇒  "oops!"
```

In the next section we will discuss Scheme expressions in more detail. Throughout this chapter, keep in mind that your Scheme system is one of the most useful tools for learning Scheme. Whenever you try one of the examples in the text, follow it up with your own examples. In an interactive system like Scheme, the cost of trying something out is relatively small— usually just the time to type it in.

2-2 Simple Expressions

The simplest Scheme expressions are data objects, such as strings, numbers, symbols, and lists. Scheme supports other object types, but these four are enough for many programs. We saw some examples of strings and numbers in the preceding section.

Let's discuss numbers in a little more detail. Numbers are constants. If you enter a number, Scheme echoes it back to you. The following examples show that Scheme supports several types of numbers.

```
1234567654321   ⇒ 1234567654321
3/4             ⇒ 3/4
2.718281828     ⇒ 2.718281828
```

Scheme provides the names +, -, *, and / for the corresponding arithmetic procedures. Each procedure takes two numeric arguments. The expressions below are called *procedure applications*, because they specify the application of a procedure to a set of arguments.

```
(+ 1/2 1/2)   ⇒ 1
(- 1.5 1/2)   ⇒ 1.0
(* 3 1/2)     ⇒ 3/2
(/ 1.5 3/4)   ⇒ 2.0
```

Scheme uses prefix notation even for common arithmetic operations. This means that any procedure application, whether the procedure takes zero, one, two, or more arguments, is written with the notation (*procedure arg* ...). This regularity simplifies the syntax of expressions; one notation is employed regardless of the operation, and there are no confusing rules regarding the precedence of operators.

Procedure applications may be nested, in which case the innermost values are computed first. So we can nest applications of the arithmetic procedures given above to evaluate more complicated formulas.

```
(+ (+ 2 2) (+ 2 2))        ⇒ 8
(- 2 (* 4 1/3))            ⇒ 2/3
(* 2 (* 2 (* 2 (* 2 2))))  ⇒ 32
(/ (* 6/7 7/2) (- 4.5 1.5)) ⇒ 1.0
```

These examples demonstrate everything you need to use Scheme as a four-function desk calculator. While we will not discuss them in this chapter, Scheme supports many other arithmetic procedures. Now might be a good time to turn to Section 5–3 and experiment with some of them.

Simple numeric objects are sufficient for many tasks, but sometimes aggregate data structures containing two or more values are needed. In many languages, the basic aggregate data structure is the array. In Scheme, it is the *list*. Lists are written as sequences of objects surrounded by parentheses. For instance, (1 2 3 4 5) is a list of numbers, and ("this" "is" "a" "list") is a list of strings. Lists are not required to hold only one type of object, so (4.2 "hi") is a valid list containing a number and a string. Lists may be nested, so ((1 2) (3 4)) is a valid list with two elements, each of which is a list of two elements.

You may notice that lists look just like procedure applications, and wonder how Scheme tells them apart. That is, how does Scheme distinguish between a list of objects, $(obj_1\ obj_2\ \ldots)$ and a procedure application, $(procedure\ arg\ \ldots)$?

In some cases, the distinction seems obvious. The list of numbers (1 2 3 4 5) could hardly be confused with a procedure application, since 1 is a number, not a procedure. So, the answer might be that Scheme looks at the first element of the list or procedure application and makes its decision based on whether that first element is a procedure or not. This answer is not good enough, since we may even want to treat a valid procedure application such as (+ 3 4) as a list. The answer is that we must tell Scheme explicitly to treat a list as data rather than as a procedure application. We do this with quote.

```
(quote (1 2 3 4 5))            ⇒ (1 2 3 4 5)
(quote ("this" "is" "a" "list")) ⇒ ("this" "is" "a" "list")
(quote (+ 3 4))                ⇒ (+ 3 4)
```

The `quote` forces the list to be treated as data. Try entering the above expressions without the quote; you should receive an error message for the first two (but of course not for the third).

Because `quote` is required fairly frequently in Scheme code, Scheme recognizes a single quote mark (') preceding an expression as an abbreviation for `quote`.

```
'(1 2 3 4)       ⇒ (1 2 3 4)
'((1 2) (3 4))   ⇒ ((1 2) (3 4))
'(/ (* 2 -1) 3)  ⇒ (/ (* 2 -1) 3)
```

Both forms are referred to as `quote` expressions. We often say an object is *quoted* when it is enclosed in a `quote` expression.

A `quote` expression is *not* a procedure application, since it inhibits the evaluation of its "argument" expression. It is an entirely different syntactic form. Scheme supports several other syntactic forms in addition to procedure applications and `quote` expressions. Each syntactic form is evaluated differently. Fortunately, the number of different syntactic forms is small. We will see more of them later in this chapter.

Not all `quote` expressions involve lists. Try the following expression with and without the `quote`.

```
(quote hello)  ⇒ hello
```

The symbol `hello` must be quoted in order to prevent Scheme from treating `hello` as an *identifier*. Symbols and identifiers in Scheme are similar to symbols and identifiers in mathematical expressions and equations. When we evaluate the mathematical expression $1 - x$ for some value of x, we think of x as an identifier. On the other hand, when we consider the algebraic equation $x^2 - 1 = (x-1)(x+1)$, we think of x as a symbol (in fact, we think of the whole equation symbolically). Just as quoting a list told Scheme to use the list as list data rather than as a procedure application, quoting a symbol tells Scheme to use it as symbolic data rather than as an identifier. While the most common use of symbols is for identifiers, symbols may also be used, for example, as words in the representation of natural language sentences.

You might wonder why the designers of Scheme (and of Lisp) chose to represent applications and identifiers with the same notation as lists and symbols. It allows Scheme programs to be Scheme data, simplifying the writing of Scheme interpreters, compilers, editors and other tools in Scheme. This is demonstrated by the Scheme interpreter given in Section 9–3, which is itself written in Scheme. Many people believe this to be one of the most important features of Scheme.

Numbers and strings may be quoted too:

```
'2                    ⇒ 2
'2/3                  ⇒ 2/3
(quote "hi mom!")   ⇒ "hi mom!"
```

However, since numbers and strings are already constants, quote is unnecessary.

Now let's discuss some Scheme procedures for manipulating lists. There are two basic procedures for taking apart lists. car returns the first element of a list, and cdr returns the remainder of the list. The names car and cdr (pronounced *could-er*) date back to the early days of Lisp programming. They were the names of machine instructions on the first computer for which a Lisp system was written. Each requires a nonempty list as its argument.

```
(car '(a b c))         ⇒ a
(cdr '(a b c))         ⇒ (b c)
(cdr '(a))             ⇒ ()
(car (cdr '(a b c)))   ⇒ b
(cdr (cdr '(a b c)))   ⇒ (c)
(car '((a b) (c d)))   ⇒ (a b)
(cdr '((a b) (c d)))   ⇒ ((c d))
```

The first element of a list is often called the car of the list, and the rest of the list is often called the cdr of the list. The cdr of a list with one element is (), the *empty list*.

The procedure cons constructs lists. It takes two arguments. The second argument is usually a list, and in that case cons returns a list.

```
(cons 'a '())                     ⇒ (a)
(cons 'a '(b c))                  ⇒ (a b c)
(cons 'a (cons 'b (cons 'c '())))  ⇒ (a b c)
(cons '(a b) '(c d))              ⇒ ((a b) c d)
(car (cons 'a '(b c)))            ⇒ a
(cdr (cons 'a '(b c)))            ⇒ (b c)
(cons (car '(a b c))
      (cdr '(a b c)))             ⇒ (a b c)
```

Just as *car* and *cdr* are often used as nouns, *cons* is often used as a verb. Creating a list by adding an element to the beginning of another list is referred to as *consing* the element onto the list.

Notice the word *usually* in the third sentence of the preceding paragraph. The procedure cons actually builds *pairs*, and there is no reason that the cdr of a pair must be a list. A list is a sequence of pairs; each pair's cdr is the next pair in the sequence. The cdr of the last pair in a *proper list* is the empty list. Otherwise, the sequence of pairs forms an *improper list*. More formally, the empty list is a proper list, and any pair whose cdr is a proper list is a proper list (and nothing else). Because of its printed representation, a pair whose cdr is not a list is often called a *dotted pair*.

```
(cons 'a 'b)         ⇒ (a . b)
(cdr '(a . b))       ⇒ b
(cons 'a '(b . c))   ⇒ (a b . c)
```

The procedure list is similar to cons, except that it takes an arbitrary number of arguments and always builds a proper list.

```
(list 'a 'b 'c)   ⇒ (a b c)
(list 'a)         ⇒ (a)
(list)            ⇒ ()
```

Section 5–2 provides more information on lists and the Scheme procedures for manipulating them. This might be a good time to turn to that section and familiarize yourself with the other procedures given there.

Exercise 2–1: Convert the following arithmetic expressions into Scheme expressions and evaluate them:

$$1.2 * (2 - 1/3) + -8.7$$

$$(2/3 + 4/9)/(5/11 - 4/3)$$

$$1 + 1/(2 + 1/(1 + 1/2))$$

$$1 * -2 * 3 * -4 * 5 * -6 * 7$$

Exercise 2–2: Experiment with the procedures +, -, *, and / to determine the Scheme's rules for the type of value returned by each when given different types of numeric arguments.

Exercise 2–3: Determine the value of the following expressions.

```
(cons 'car 'cdr)
(list 'this '(is silly))
(cons 'is '(this silly?))

(quote (+ 2 3))
(cons '+ '(2 3))
(car '(+ 2 3))
(cdr '(+ 2 3))

cons
(quote cons)
(quote (quote cons))
(car (quote (quote cons)))

(+ 2 3)
(+ '2 '3)
(+ (car '(2 3)) (car (cdr '(2 3))))
((car (list + - * /)) 2 3)
```

Exercise 2–4: (car (car '((a b) (c d)))) yields a. Determine what compositions of car and cdr yield b, c, and d.

Exercise 2–5: If you type the expression (car (car (car '((a b) (c d))))), Scheme will signal an error, because (car '((a b) (c d))) is (a b), (car '(a b)) is a, and (car 'a) is undefined. Determine all legal compositions of car and cdr applied to ((a b) (c d)).

2-3 Evaluating Scheme Expressions

Let's turn to a discussion of how Scheme evaluates the expressions you type. We have already established the rule for constant objects such as strings and numbers; the object itself is the value. You have probably also worked out in your mind a rule for evaluating procedure applications of the form (*procedure arg$_1$ ... arg$_n$*). Here, *procedure* is an expression representing a Scheme procedure, and *arg$_1$ ... arg$_n$* are expressions representing its arguments. One possibility is the following:

- Find the value of *procedure*.
- Find the value of *arg$_1$*.
  ⋮

- Find the value of arg_n.
- Apply the value of *procedure* to the values of $arg_1 \ldots arg_n$.

For example, consider the simple procedure application (+ 3 4). The value of + is the addition procedure, the value of 3 is the number 3, and the value of 4 is the number 4. Applying the addition procedure to 3 and 4 yields 7, so our value is the object 7.

By performing this process recursively, we can find the value of the nested expression (* (+ 3 4) 2). The value of * is the multiplication procedure, the value of (+ 3 4) we can determine recursively to be the number 7, and the value of 2 is the number 2. Multiplying 7 by 2 we get 14, so our answer is the object 14.

This rule works for procedure applications but, unfortunately, not for quote expressions. This is because the subexpressions of a procedure application are evaluated, while the subexpressions of a quote expression are not. The evaluation of a quote expression is more similar to the evaluation of constant objects. The value of a quote expression of the form (quote *object*) is simply *object*.

Constant objects, procedure applications, and quote expressions are only three of the many syntactic forms provided by Scheme. Fortunately, only a few of the other syntactic forms need to be handled directly by a Scheme evaluator; these are referred to as *core* syntactic forms. The remaining syntactic forms are *syntactic extensions* defined, ultimately, in terms of the core syntactic forms. We will discuss the remaining core syntactic forms and a few syntactic extensions in the remaining sections of this chapter. Section 2–10 summarizes the core syntactic forms and introduces the syntactic extension mechanism.

Before we go on to learn more syntactic forms and procedures, two points related to the evaluation of procedure applications are worthy of note. First, the process given above is too restrictive, in that it requires the subexpressions to be evaluated from left to right. That is, *procedure* is evaluated before arg_1, arg_1 is evaluated before arg_2, and so on. This need not be the case. Any Scheme evaluator is free to evaluate the expressions in any order—left to right, right to left, or anything in between. In fact, the subexpressions may be evaluated in different orders for different applications even in the same implementation.

The second point is that *procedure* is evaluated in the same manner as $arg_1 \ldots arg_n$. While *procedure* often is an identifier that names a particular procedure, this need not be the case. One of the exercises in the previous section had you determine the value of ((car (list + - * /)) 2 3). Here, *procedure* is (car (list + - * /)). The value of (car (list + - * /)) is the addition procedure, just as if *procedure* were simply the identifier +.

Exercise 2–6: Write down the steps necessary to evaluate each of the following expressions.

```
((car (cdr (list + - * /))) 17 5)
(cons (quote -) (cdr (quote (+ b c))))
(cdr (cdr '(a b c)))
(cons 'd (cddr '(a b c d e f)))
(cons (+ '2 1/2) (list (- '3 1/3) (+ '4 1/4)))
```

2-4 Identifiers and Let Expressions

Suppose *expr* is a Scheme expression that contains an identifier *id*. Suppose, additionally, that we would like *id* to have the value *val* when we evaluate *expr*. For example, we might like x to have the value 2 when we evaluate (+ x 3). Or, we might want y to have the value 3 when we evaluate (+ 2 y). The following examples demonstrate how to do this using Scheme's let syntactic form.

```
(let ([x 2])
   (+ x 3))         ⇒ 5
(let ([y 3])
   (+ 2 y))         ⇒ 5
(let ([x 2] [y 3])
   (+ x y))         ⇒ 5
```

The let syntactic form includes a list of identifier-value pairs, along with a sequence of expressions referred to as the body of the let. The general form is

```
(let ([id val] ...) exp₁ exp₂ ...).
```

By convention, we use brackets ([ ]) around each identifier-value pair rather than parentheses. We say the identifiers are *bound* to the values by the let. We refer to identifiers bound by let as *let-bound* identifiers.

A let expression is often used to simplify an expression that would contain two identical subexpressions. This not only simplifies the expression but also ensures that the value of the common subexpression is computed only once.

```
(+ (* 4 4) (* 4 4))  ⇒ 32
(let ([a (* 4 4)])
    (+ a a))              ⇒ 32

(let ([list1 '(a b c)] [list2 '(d e f)])
    (cons (cons (car list1)
                (car list2))
          (cons (car (cdr list1))
                (car (cdr list2)))))        ⇒ ((a . d) b . e)
```

Since expressions in the first position of a procedure application are evaluated no differently from other expressions, a let-bound identifier may be used there as well.

```
(let ([f +])
    (f 2 3))                 ⇒ 5
(let ([f +] [x 2])
    (f x 3))                 ⇒ 5
(let ([f +] [x 2] [y 3])
    (f x y))                 ⇒ 5
```

The identifiers bound by let are visible only within the body of the let.

```
(let ([+ *])
    (+ 2 3))   ⇒ 6
(+ 2 3)         ⇒ 5
```

This is fortunate, because we do not want to change the value of + to the multiplication procedure everywhere.

It is possible to nest let expressions.

```
(let ([a 4] [b -3])
    (let ([a-squared (* a a)]
          [b-squared (* b b)])
        (+ a-squared b-squared)))   ⇒ 25
```

The syntactic form let* is a shorthand for nested let expressions. With let, the set of bindings are all made at the same time, after the values have been computed. With let*, the bindings are made sequentially from first to last (left to right, looking at the let* expression as if it were all on one line). Each value may depend on the values computed before it. That is, each value is within the scope of the identifiers that come before it.

```
(let* ([a 4]
       [b -3]
       [a-squared (* a a)]
       [b-squared (* b b)])
   (+ a-squared b-squared))   ⇒ 25
```

When nested let expressions bind the same identifier, only the binding created by the inner let is visible within its body.

```
(let ([x 1])
   (let ([x (+ x 1)])
      (+ x 2)))          ⇒ 4
```

The outer let expression binds x to 1 within its body, which is the second let expression. The inner let expression binds x to (+ x 1) within its body, which is the expression (+ x 2). What is the value of (+ x 1)? Since (+ x 1) appears within the body of the outer let but not within the body of the inner let, the value of x must be 1 and hence the value of (+ x 1) is 2. What about (+ x 2)? It appears within the body of both let expressions. Only the inner binding for x is visible, so x is 2 and (+ x 2) is 4.

The inner binding for x is said to *shadow* the outer binding. A let-bound identifier is visible everywhere within the body of its let expression except where it is shadowed. The region where an identifier binding is visible is called its *scope*. The scope of the first x in the example above is the body of the outer let expression minus the body of the second let expression, where it is shadowed by the second x.

In general, shadowing may be avoided by choosing different names for identifiers. The expression above could be rewritten so that the identifier bound by the inner let is y.

```
(let ([x 1])
   (let ([y (+ x 1)])
      (+ y 2)))          ⇒ 4
```

Although shadowing is sometimes convenient, it is often best to avoid confusion by choosing different names.

By the way, we can still use let* as an abbreviation for nested let expressions that bind the same identifier name.

```
(let* ([x 1] [x (+ x 1)])
  (+ x 2))                    ⇒ 4
```

This may look strange, but it is entirely equivalent to the earlier version written with let. Of course, it is less confusing (and therefore better programming practice) to use two different names in this example.

Exercise 2–7: Rewrite the following expressions using let to remove common subexpressions and to improve the structure of the code. Do not perform any algebraic simplifications.

```
(+ (- (* 3 a) b) (+ (* 3 a) b))
(cons (car (list a b c)) (cdr (list a b c)))
```

Exercise 2–8: Determine the value of the following expression. Explain how you derived this value.

```
(let ([x 9])
  (* x
     (let ([x (/ x 3)])
       (+ x x))))
```

Exercise 2–9: Rewrite the following expressions to give unique names to each different let-bound identifier so that none of the identifiers is shadowed. Verify that the value of your expression is the same as that of the original expression.

```
(let ([x 'a] [y 'b])
  (list (let ([x 'c]) (cons x y))
        (let ([y 'd]) (cons x y))))
(let ([x '((a b) c)])
  (cons (let ([x (cdr x)])
          (car x))
        (let ([x (car x)])
          (cons (let ([x (cdr x)])
                  (car x))
                (cons (let ([x (car x)])
```

```
          x)
    (cdr x))))))
```

2-5 Lambda Expressions

In the expression (let ([x (* 3 4)]) (+ x x)), the identifier x is bound to the value of (* 3 4). What if we would like the value of (+ x x) where x is bound to the value of (/ 99 11)? Where x is bound to the value of (- 2 7)? In each case we need a different let expression. However, when the body of the let is complicated, having to retype it can be inconvenient.

Instead, we can use the syntactic form lambda to create a new procedure that has x as a parameter and has the same body as the let expression.

    (lambda (x) (+ x x))   ⇒ #<procedure>

The general form of a lambda expression is

    (lambda (id ...) exp₁ exp₂ ...).

The identifiers (id ...) are the *formal parameters* of the procedure, and the sequence of expressions exp_1 exp_2 ... is its body. (Actually, the true general form is somewhat more general than this, as you will see at the end of this section.)

A procedure is just as much an object as a number, string, symbol, or pair. However, it does not have any meaningful printed representation as far as Scheme is concerned, so this book uses the notation #<procedure> to show that the value of an expression is a procedure.

The most common operation to perform on a procedure is to apply it to one or more values.

    ((lambda (x) (+ x x)) (* 3 4))   ⇒ 24

This is nothing more than a procedure application. The procedure is the value of (lambda (x) (+ x x)), and the only argument is the value of (* 3 4), or 12. The argument values, or *actual parameters*, are bound to the formal parameters within the body of the lambda expression in the same way as let-bound identifiers are bound to their values. In this case, x is bound to 12. The value of (+ x x) is thus 24. The value of the procedure, given the value 12, is 24.

The reader may be wondering at this point why bother with a lambda expression when the corresponding let expression is actually shorter. The answer is that, because procedures are objects, we can establish a procedure as the value of an identifier and use the procedure more than once.

```
(let ([double (lambda (x) (+ x x))])
  (list (double (* 3 4))
        (double (/ 99 11))
        (double (- 2 7))))          ⇒ (24 18 -10)
```

Here, we establish a binding for double to a procedure, then use this procedure to double three different values.

The procedure expects its actual parameter to be a number, since it passes the actual parameter on to +. In general, the actual parameter may be any sort of object. Consider, for example, a similar procedure that uses cons instead of +.

```
(let ([double-cons (lambda (x) (cons x x))])
  (double-cons 'a))                 ⇒ (a . a)
```

Noting the similarity between double and double-cons, you should not be surprised to learn that they may be collapsed into a single procedure by adding an additional argument.

```
(let ([double-any (lambda (f x) (f x x))])
  (list (double-any + 13)
        (double-any cons 'a)))      ⇒ (26 (a . a))
```

This demonstrates not only that procedures may accept more than one argument, but also that an argument passed to a procedure may itself be a procedure.

As with let expressions, lambda expressions become somewhat more interesting when they are nested within other lambda or let expressions.

```
(let ([x 'a])
  (let ([f (lambda (y) (list x y))])
    (f 'b)))                        ⇒ (a b)
```

The occurrence of x within the lambda expression refers to the x outside the lambda that is bound by the outer let expression. The identifier x is said to *occur free* in the lambda expression. The identifier y does not occur free in the lambda expression since it is bound by the lambda expression. An identifier that occurs free in a lambda expression should be bound by an enclosing lambda or let expression, unless it is (like the names of primitive procedures) bound at top-level as we discuss in the following section.

What happens when the procedure is applied somewhere outside of the scope of the bindings for identifiers that occur free within the procedure, as in the following expression?

```
(let ([f (let ([x 'a])
           (lambda (y) (cons x y)))])
  (f 'b))                              ⇒ (a . b)
```

The answer is that the same bindings that were in effect when the procedure was created are in effect again when the procedure is applied. This is so, even if there is another binding for x that is visible where the procedure is applied.

```
(let ([f (let ([x 'a])
           (lambda (y) (cons x y)))])
  (let ([x 'i-am-not-a])
    (f 'b)))                           ⇒ (a . b)
```

In both cases, the value of x within the procedure named f is a.

Incidentally, a let expression is nothing more than the direct application of a lambda expression to a set of argument expressions. For example, the two expressions below are equivalent:

```
(let ([x 'a])
  (cons x x))
((lambda (x) (cons x x))
 'a)
```

In fact, a let expression is a syntactic extension defined in terms of lambda and procedure application, which are both core syntactic forms. In general, any expression of the form

```
(let ([id val] ...) exp₁ exp₂ ...)
```

is expanded into an expression of the form

```
((lambda (id ...) exp₁ exp₂ ...)
 val ...)
```

See Section 2–10 or Section 8–1 for details.

As was mentioned above, the general form for lambda is a bit more complicated than the form we saw earlier, in that the identifier list, (*id* ...), need not be a proper list, or indeed even a list at all. The "identifier list" can be in any one of the following three forms:

1 A proper list of identifiers, (*id* ...), such as we have already seen,

2 A single identifier, *id*, or

3 An improper list of identifiers, (id_1 id_2 ... . id_3).

In the first case, the number of arguments must correspond exactly to the number of identifiers. Each identifier is bound to the corresponding argument. In the second, any number of arguments is valid; all of the arguments are put into a single list and the single identifier is bound to this list. In the third case, if there are n identifiers id_1 id_2 ..., *i.e.*, excluding id_3, there must be at least n arguments. Each of these n identifiers is bound to the corresponding argument; all of the arguments beyond the nth are put into a list and the identifier id_3 is bound to this list.

Let's consider a few examples to help clarify the more general syntax of lambda expressions.

```
(let ([f (lambda x x)])
  (f 1 2 3 4))                    ⇒ (1 2 3 4)
(let ([f (lambda x x)])
  (f))                           ⇒ ()
(let ([g (lambda (x . y) (list x y))])
  (g 1 2 3 4))                   ⇒ (1 (2 3 4))
(let ([h (lambda (x y . z) (list x y z))])
  (h 'a 'b 'c 'd))              ⇒ (a b (c d))
```

In the first two examples, the procedure named f accepts any number of arguments. These arguments are automatically formed into a list to which the identifier x is bound; the value of f is this list. In the first example, the arguments are 1, 2, 3, and 4, so the answer is (1 2 3 4). In the second, there are no arguments, so the answer is the empty list (). The value of the procedure named g in the third example is a list whose first element is the first argument and whose second element is a list containing the remaining arguments. The procedure named h is similar but separates out the second argument. While f accepts any number of arguments, g must have at least one and h must have at least two.

Exercise 2–10: Determine the value of the expressions below.

```
(let ([f (lambda (x) x)])
  (f 'a))
(let ([f (lambda x x)])
  (f 'a))
```

```
(let ([f (lambda (x . y) x)])
   (f 'a))
```

Exercise 2–11: How might the primitive procedure `list` be defined?

Exercise 2–12: List the identifiers that occur free in each of the `lambda` expressions below. Do not omit identifiers that name primitive procedures such as + or `cons`.

```
(lambda (f x) (f x))
(lambda (x) (+ x x))
(lambda (x y) (f x y))
(lambda (x)
   (cons x (f x y)))
(lambda (x)
   (let ([y (cons x y)])
      (list x y z)))
```

2-6 Top-Level Definitions

The identifiers bound by `let` and `lambda` expressions are not visible outside of the bodies of these expressions. Suppose you have created an object, perhaps a procedure, that must be accessible anywhere, like + or `cons`. What you need is a *top-level definition*, which may be established with `define`. Top-level definitions are visible in every expression you enter, except where shadowed by another binding.

Let's establish a top-level definition for the `double-any` procedure of the last section.

```
(define double-any
   (lambda (f x)
      (f x x)))
```

The identifier `double-any` now has the same status as `cons` or the name of any other primitive procedure. We can now use `double-any` as if it were a primitive procedure.

```
(double-any + 10)     ⇒ 20
(double-any cons 'a)  ⇒ (a . a)
```

A top-level definition may be established for any object, not just for procedures.

```
(define sandwich "peanut-butter-and-jelly")
```

```
sandwich  ⇒ "peanut-butter-and-jelly"
```

Most often, though, top-level definitions are used for procedures.

As suggested above, top-level definitions may be shadowed by `let` or `lambda` bindings.

```
(define xyz '(x y z))
(let ([xyz '(z y x)])
   xyz)                 ⇒ (z y x)
```

Identifiers with top-level definitions act almost as if they were bound by a `let` expression enclosing all of the expressions you type.

Given only the simple tools you have read about up to this point, it is already possible to define some of the primitive procedures provided by Scheme and described later in this book. If you completed the exercises from the last section, you should already know how to define `list`.

```
(define list
   (lambda x x))
```

Also, Scheme provides the abbreviations `cadr` and `cddr` for the composition of `car` with `cdr` and `cdr` with `cdr`. That is, (`cadr` *list*) is equivalent to (`car` (`cdr` *list*)), and similarly, (`cddr` *list*) is equivalent to (`cdr` (`cdr` *list*)). They are easily defined as follows:

```
(define cadr
   (lambda (x)
      (car (cdr x))))
(define cddr
   (lambda (x)
      (cdr (cdr x))))
```

```
(cadr '(a b c))  ⇒ b
(cddr '(a b c))  ⇒ (c)
```

Top-level definitions make it easier for us to experiment with a procedure, because we need not retype the procedure each time it is used. Let's try defining a somewhat more complicated variation of double-any, one that turns an "ordinary" two-argument procedure into a "doubling" one-argument procedure.

```
(define doubler
  (lambda (f)
    (lambda (x) (f x x))))
```

The procedure doubler takes a procedure f as its argument. The value of doubler is a new procedure that takes an object and applies f to two of the object. We can now define the simple double and double-cons procedures of the last section:

```
(define double (doubler +))
(double 13/2)                        ⇒ 13
(define double-cons (doubler cons))
(double-cons 'a)                     ⇒ (a . a)
```

We can also define double-any with doubler:

```
(define double-any
  (lambda (f x)
    ((doubler f) x)))
```

Within double and double-cons, f retains the appropriate value, *i.e.*, + or cons, even though the procedures are clearly applied outside the scope of f.

What happens if you attempt to use an identifier that is not bound by a let or lambda expression and that does not have a top-level definition? Try using the identifier i-am-not-defined to see what happens:

```
(i-am-not-defined 3)
```

Scheme should print an error message to inform you that the identifier is not defined.

However, there is one circumstance in which Scheme will not complain about the use of an undefined identifier. This is when you use it within a lambda expression. The following should *not* cause an error, even though we have not yet established a top-level definition for proc2.

```
(define proc1
  (lambda (x y)
    (proc2 y x)))
```

If you try to use proc1 before defining proc2, you should get an error message. Let's give proc2 a top-level definition and try proc1.

```
(define proc2 cons)
(proc1 'a 'b)          ⇒ (b . a)
```

When you define proc1, Scheme accepts your promise to define proc2, and does not complain unless you use proc1 before defining proc2. This allows you to define procedures in any order you please. This is especially useful when you are trying to organize a file full of procedure definitions in a way that makes your program more readable. It is necessary when two procedures defined at top level depend upon each other; we will see some examples of this later.

Exercise 2–13: What would happen if you typed

```
(double-any double-any double-any),
```

given the definition of double-any from the beginning of this section?

Exercise 2–14: A more elegant way to define cadr and cddr than given in this section is to define a procedure that composes two procedures to create a third. Write the procedure compose, such that (compose $proc_1$ $proc_2$) is the composition of $proc_1$ and $proc_2$ (assuming both take one argument). Use compose to define cadr and cddr.

Exercise 2–15: Scheme also provides caar, cdar, caaar, caadr, and so on, with any combination of up to four a's (representing car) and d's (representing cdr) between the c and the r (see Section 5–2). Define each of these with the compose procedure of the previous exercise.

2-7 Conditional Expressions

So far we have considered expressions that perform a given task unconditionally. Suppose that we wish to write the procedure abs, whose value is the absolute value of its argument. The most straightforward way to write abs is to first determine whether the argument is negative or not, using the if syntactic form.

```
(define abs
   (lambda (n)
      (if (< n 0)
          (- 0 n)
          n)))
(abs 77)              ⇒ 77
(abs -77)             ⇒ 77
```

An if expression has the general form (if *test consequent alternative*). *Consequent* is the value to return if *test* is true; *alternative* is the value to return if *test* is false. In the expression above, *test* is (< n 0), *consequent* is (- 0 n), and *alternative* is n.

The procedure abs could be written in a variety of other ways. Any of the following are valid definitions for abs.

```
(define abs
   (lambda (n)
      (if (>= n 0)
          n
          (- 0 n))))
(define abs
   (lambda (n)
      (if (not (< n 0))
          n
          (- 0 n))))
(define abs
   (lambda (n)
      (if (or (> n 0) (= n 0))
          n
          (- 0 n))))
(define abs
   (lambda (n)
      (if (= n 0)
          0
          (if (< n 0)
              (- 0 n)
              n)))))
(define abs
   (lambda (n)
```

```
((if (>= n 0) + -)
 0
 n)))
```

The first of these alternate definitions asks if n is greater than or equal to zero, inverting the test. The second asks if n is not less than zero, using the procedure not with <. The third asks if n is greater than zero or n is equal to zero, using the syntactic form or. The fourth treats zero separately, though there is no benefit in doing so. The fifth is somewhat tricky; n is either added to or subtracted from zero, depending upon whether n is greater than or equal to zero.

Why is if a syntactic form and not a procedure? In order to answer this, let's look again at the definition of reciprocal from the first section of this chapter.

```
(define reciprocal
   (lambda (n)
      (if (= n 0)
          "oops!"
          (/ 1 n))))
```

When Scheme is asked to divide anything by zero, it signals an error. The definition of reciprocal avoids the error by testing first if its argument is zero. But if if were a procedure, its arguments (including (/ 1 n)) would be evaluated before it had a chance to choose between the consequent and alternative. Like quote, which does not evaluate its only subexpression, if does not evaluate all of its subexpressions and so cannot be a procedure.

The syntactic form or operates in a manner similar to if. The general form of an or expression is (or *exp* ...). If there are no subexpressions, *i.e.*, the expression is simply (or), the value is false. Otherwise, each *exp* is evaluated in turn until either (a) one of them is true, or (b) there are no more left. In case (a), the value is true; in case (b), the value is false.

To be more precise, in either case (a) or (b), the value of the or expression is the value of the last subexpression evaluated. This clarification is necessary because there is not just a single true value, nor a single false value. Usually, the value of a test expression is one of the two objects #t, for true, or #f, for false.

```
(< -1 0)  ⇒ #t
(> -1 0)  ⇒ #f
```

However, every Scheme object is considered to be either true or false by the conditional expressions if and or and by the procedure not. Only one object besides #f is considered false; this is the empty list (). (In many Scheme systems, #f *is* (), *i.e.*, if you type in #f, the value returned by Scheme will be ().) All other objects are considered true. This is why it is meaningful in the description of or above to say that, in case (a), the value of or is the value of the first true expression and that, in case (b), the value of or is the value of the last expression.

```
(not #t)          ⇒ #f
(not #f)          ⇒ #t
(not '())         ⇒ #t

(not 1)           ⇒ #f
(not '(a b c))    ⇒ #f

(or)              ⇒ #f
(or #f)           ⇒ #f
(or #f #t)        ⇒ #t
(or #f 'a #f)     ⇒ a
```

The and syntactic form is similar in form to or, but an and expression is true if all its subexpressions are true, and false otherwise. In the case where there are no subexpressions, *i.e.*, the expression is simply (and), the value is true. Otherwise, the subexpressions are evaluated in turn until either there are no more subexpressions or the value of a subexpression is false. In either case, the value is the value of the last subexpression evaluated.

Using and, we can define a slightly different version of reciprocal.

```
(define reciprocal
   (lambda (n)
      (and (not (= n 0))
           (/ 1 n))))
(reciprocal 3)              ⇒ 1/3
(reciprocal 0.5)           ⇒ 2.0
(reciprocal 0)             ⇒ #f
```

In this version, value is #f if n is zero, 1/n otherwise.

The procedures =, <, >, <=, and >= are called *predicates*. A predicate is a procedure that answers a specific question about its arguments and returns one of the two values #t or #f. The names of most predicates end with a question mark (?); the common numeric procedures listed above are the only exceptions to this rule. Not all predicates require numeric arguments, of course. The predicate null? returns true if its argument is the empty list (), false otherwise.

```
(null? '())               ⇒ #t
(null? 'abc)              ⇒ #f
(null? '(x y z))          ⇒ #f
(null? (cdddr '(x y z)))  ⇒ #t
```

Ordinarily, if you pass the procedure cdr anything other than a pair, including the empty list (), Scheme signals an error. However, in many Lisp dialects, (cdr '()) returns (). The following procedure, lisp-cdr, is a variant of cdr whose value is () if the argument is ().

```
(define lisp-cdr
    (lambda (x)
        (if (null? x)
            '()
            (cdr x))))
```

Another useful predicate is equal?, which takes two arguments. If the two arguments have the same structure, equal? returns true. Otherwise, equal? returns false.

```
(equal? 'a 'a)            ⇒ #t
(equal? 'a 'b)            ⇒ #f
(equal? '(a b c) '(a b c)) ⇒ #t
(equal? '(a b c) '(c b a)) ⇒ #f
(equal? "hi" "mom!")      ⇒ #f
```

There is also a class of *type predicates* that return true or false depending on the type of the object, *e.g.*, pair?, symbol?, number?, and string?. The predicate pair?, for example, returns true only if its argument is a pair.

```
(pair? '(a . c))     ⇒ #t
(pair? '(a b c))     ⇒ #t
(pair? '())          ⇒ #f
(pair? 'abc)         ⇒ #f
(pair? "hi mom!")    ⇒ #f
(pair? 1234567890)   ⇒ #f
```

Type predicates are useful for deciding if the argument passed to a procedure is of the appropriate type. For example, the following version of reciprocal checks first to see that its argument is a number before testing against zero or performing the division.

```
(define reciprocal
   (lambda (n)
      (if (and (number? n) (not (= n 0)))
          (/ 1 n)
          "oops!")))
```

By the way, the code that uses reciprocal must check to see that the returned value is a number and not a string. It is usually better to report
the error, using whatever error-reporting facilities your Scheme system has.
Chez Scheme provides the procedure error for reporting errors; see Section 7–8 for details.

   Let's consider one more conditional expression, cond, that is often useful
in place of if. A cond expression is similar to if except it allows multiple
test and alternative expressions. A cond expression usually takes the form

      (cond [*test exp*] ... [else *exp*]).

Brackets are used, as with let, merely to help show the structure of the
expression; parentheses may be used instead. Recall the definition for abs
that employed two if expressions:

```
(define abs
   (lambda (n)
      (if (= n 0)
          0
          (if (< n 0)
              (- 0 n)
              n))))
```

The two if expressions may be replaced by a single cond expression as
follows.

```
(define abs
   (lambda (n)
      (cond
         [(= n 0) 0]
         [(< n 0) (- 0 n)]
         [else n])))
```

Sometimes it is clearer to leave out the else clause. This should be done
only when there is no possibility that all the tests will fail, as in the new
definition for abs below.

```
(define abs
   (lambda (n)
      (cond
         [(= n 0) 0]
         [(< n 0) (- 0 n)]
         [(> n 0) n])))
```

These definitions for abs do not depend on the order in which the tests were performed, since only one of the tests can be true for any value of n. The following procedure computes the tax on a given amount of income in a progressive tax system with breakpoints at 10,000, 20,000, and 30,000 dollars.

```
(define income-tax
   (lambda (income)
      (cond
         [(<= income 10000)
          (* income .05)]
         [(<= income 20000)
          (+ (* (- income 10000) .08)
             500.00)]
         [(<= income 30000)
          (+ (* (- income 20000) .13)
             1300.00)]
         [else
          (+ (* (- income 30000) .21)
             2600.00)])))
```

```
(income-tax 5000)    ⇒  250.0
(income-tax 15000)   ⇒  900.0
(income-tax 25000)   ⇒  1950.0
(income-tax 50000)   ⇒  6800.0
```

Exercise 2–16: Scheme provides the procedures min and max. Each takes two numeric arguments. The procedure min returns the minimum of the two arguments, or the first if they are equal; max returns the maximum, or the first if they are equal. Define min and max.

Exercise 2–17: Define the predicate list?, which returns true if its argument is a list and false otherwise. [*Hint:* The argument need not be a proper list, so it is sufficient to ask if the argument is a pair or ().]

2-8 Simple Recursion

All forms of repetition in Scheme are implemented with *recursion*. Recursion is a simple concept: the application of a procedure from within that procedure. It can be tricky to master recursion at first, but once mastered it provides expressive power far beyond ordinary looping constructs.

A *recursive procedure* is a procedure that applies itself. Perhaps the simplest recursive procedure is the following, which we will call **goodbye**.

```
(define goodbye
    (lambda ()
        (goodbye)))
(goodbye)            ⇒
```

This procedure takes no arguments and simply applies itself immediately. There is no value after the ⇒ because **goodbye** never returns.

Obviously, to make practical use out of a recursive procedure, we must have some way to terminate the recursion. Most recursive procedures should have at least two basic elements, a *base case* and a *recursion step*. The base case terminates the recursion, giving the value of the procedure for some base argument. The recursion step gives the value in terms of the value of the procedure applied to a different argument. In order for the recursion to terminate, the different argument must be closer to the base argument in some way.

Let's consider the problem of finding the length of a list recursively. We need a base case and a recursion step. The logical base argument for recursion on lists is always the empty list. The length of the empty list is zero, so the base case should give the value zero for the empty list. In order to become closer to the empty list, the natural recursion step involves the cdr of the argument. A nonempty list is always one element longer than the cdr of the list, so the natural recursion step gives the value as one more than the length of the cdr of the list.

```
(define length
    (lambda (ls)
        (if (null? ls)
            0
            (+ (length (cdr ls)) 1))))
```

```
(length '())     ⇒ 0
(length '(a))    ⇒ 1
(length '(a b)) ⇒ 2
```

The if asks if the list is empty. If so, the value is zero. This is the base case. If not, the value is one more than the length of the cdr of the list. This is the recursion step.

Most Scheme systems allow you to trace the execution of a procedure to see how it operates. In *Chez* Scheme, all you have to do is type (trace *name*) (see Section 7–7), where *name* is the name of a procedure you have defined. If you trace length and pass it the argument '(a b c), you should see something like this:

```
(length (a b c))
|   (length (b c))
|   |   (length (c))
|   |   |   (length ())
|   |   |   0
|   |   1
|   2
3
```

The indentation shows the nesting level of the recursion; the vertical lines associate applications with their values. Notice that on each application of length the list gets smaller until it finally reaches (). The value at () is 0, and each outer layer adds 1 to arrive at the final answer of 3.

The procedure list-copy returns a copy of its argument, which must be a list. That is, list-copy returns a new list consisting of the elements (but not the pairs) of the old list.

```
(list-copy '())       ⇒ ()
(list-copy '(a b c)) ⇒ (a b c)
```

See if you can define list-copy before looking at the definition below.

```
(define list-copy
   (lambda (ls)
      (if (null? ls)
          '()
          (cons (car ls)
                (list-copy (cdr ls)))))))
```

The definition of list-copy is similar to the definition of length. The test in the base case is the same, (null? ls). However, the value in the base case is (), not 0, because we are building up a list, not a number. The recursive call is the same, but instead of adding one, list-copy conses the car of the list onto the value of the recursive call.

There is no reason why there cannot be more than one base case. The procedure member takes two arguments, an object and a list. It returns the first tail of the list whose car is equal to the object, or #f if the object is not found in the list. The value of member may be used as a list or as a truth value in a conditional expression.

```
(define member
    (lambda (x ls)
        (cond
            [(null? ls) #f]
            [(equal? (car ls) x) ls]
            [else (member x (cdr ls))]))))
```

```
(member 'a '(a b b d))        ⇒ (a b b d)
(member 'b '(a b b d))        ⇒ (b b d)
(member 'c '(a b b d))        ⇒ #f
(member 'd '(a b b d))        ⇒ (d)
(if (member 'b '(a b b d))
    "yes"
    "no")                     ⇒ "yes"
```

Here there are two conditions to check, hence the use of cond. The first condition checks for the base value of (); no object is a member of (), so the answer is #f. The second condition asks if the car of the list is the object, in this case the list is returned; it is itself the first tail whose car is equal to the object. The recursion step just continues down the list.

There may also be more than one recursion case. Like member, the procedure remove takes two arguments, an object and a list. It returns a new list with all occurrences of the object removed from the list.

```
(define remove
    (lambda (x ls)
        (cond
            [(null? ls) '()]
            [(equal? (car ls) x)
             (remove x (cdr ls))]
```

```
[else
 (cons (car ls)
       (remove x (cdr ls)))]))))

(remove 'a '(a b b d))  ⇒  (b b d)
(remove 'b '(a b b d))  ⇒  (a d)
(remove 'c '(a b b d))  ⇒  (a b b d)
(remove 'd '(a b b d))  ⇒  (a b b)
```

This definition is similar to the definition for member above, except remove does not quit once it finds the element in the car of the list. Rather, it continues on, simply ignoring the element. If the element is not found in the car of the list, remove does the same thing as list-copy above: it conses the car of the list onto the recursive value.

Up to now, the recursion has been only on the cdr of a list. It is sometimes useful, however, for a procedure to be recursive on the car as well as the cdr of the list. The procedure tree-copy looks at a structure of pairs as a tree rather than a list, with the left subtree being the car of the pair and the right subtree being the cdr of the pair. It performs a similar operation to list-copy, building new pairs while leaving the elements (leaves) alone.

```
(define tree-copy
  (lambda (tr)
    (if (not (pair? tr))
        tr
        (cons (tree-copy (car tr))
              (tree-copy (cdr tr))))))

(tree-copy '((a . b) . c))  ⇒  ((a . b) . c)
```

The natural base argument for a tree structure is anything that is not a pair, since the recursion traverses pairs rather than lists. The recursive step in this case is *doubly recursive*, finding the recursive value for the car as well as the cdr of the argument.

At this point, readers who are familiar with other languages that provide special looping constructs, *e.g.*, *while* or *for* loops, may wonder how Scheme supports them. The answer is simple. Some recursive procedure applications are essentially the same as loops and execute as such, so there is no need for special looping constructs. Furthermore, recursive definitions are often clearer because they do not involve assignments, which are necessary in traditional looping constructs and which are often difficult to follow. Section 4–5 describes the situations in which a recursive application is essentially a loop. Usually, there is no need to make a distinction, since any procedure application is relatively inexpensive. Concentrate instead on writing clear, concise, and correct programs.

Before we leave the topic of recursion, let's consider a special form of recursion called *mapping*. Consider the following procedure, abs-all, that takes a list of numbers as input and returns a list of their absolute values.

```
(define abs-all
   (lambda (ls)
      (if (null? ls)
          '()
          (cons (abs (car ls))
                (abs-all (cdr ls)))))))
```

```
(abs-all '(1 -2 3 -4 5 -6))   ⇒ (1 2 3 4 5 6)
```

This procedure returns a new list from the input list by applying the procedure abs to each element. We say that abs-all *maps* abs over the input list to produce the output list. Mapping a procedure over a list is a fairly common thing to do, so Scheme provides the procedure map, which takes the procedure to map and the list to map over as arguments. We can use map to define abs-all:

```
(define abs-all
   (lambda (ls)
      (map abs ls)))
```

However, we really do not need abs-all, since the corresponding direct application of map is just as short and perhaps clearer.

```
(map abs '(1 -2 3 -4 5 -6))   ⇒ (1 2 3 4 5 6)
```

Of course, we can use lambda to create the procedure argument to map, if we need to, for example to square the numbers in a list of numbers:

```
(map (lambda (x) (* x x))
     '(1 -3 -5 7))            ⇒ (1 9 25 49)
```

We can map a multiargument procedure over multiple lists, as in the following example:

```
(map cons '(a b c) '(1 2 3))   ⇒ ((a . 1) (b . 2) (c . 3))
```

The lists must be of the same length, and the procedure must expect as many arguments as there are lists. Each element of the output list is the result of applying the procedure to corresponding members of the input list.

Looking at the first definition of abs-all above, you should be able to derive the following definition for map1, a restricted version of map that maps a one-argument procedure over a single list, before looking at it.

```
(define map1
   (lambda (f ls)
      (if (null? ls)
          '()
          (cons (f (car ls))
                (map1 f (cdr ls)))))))
```

All we have done is to make the procedure to apply a parameter, f, and replaced the application of abs with an application of f. A definition for the more general map is given in Section 4–5.

Exercise 2–18: The predicate list? checks to see that its argument is either a pair or the empty list, but does not inspect the list to verify that it is a proper list, *i.e.*, terminated by (). Define a predicate proper-list? that returns true if its argument is a proper list and false otherwise. Try to avoid using if; use and and or instead.

Exercise 2–19: Consult Section 5–2 for the descriptions of list-ref, list-tail, and last-pair, then define them.

Exercise 2–20: Describe what would happen if you switched the order of the arguments to cons in the definition of tree-copy.

Exercise 2–21: The procedure make-list takes a nonnegative integer n and an object and returns a new list, n long, each element of which is the object. Define make-list. [*Hint:* The base test should be (= n 0), and the recursion step should involve (- n 1).] Whereas () is the natural base case for recursion on lists, 0 is the natural base case for recursion on nonnegative integers. Similarly, subtracting 1 is the natural way to bring a nonnegative integer closer to 0.

Exercise 2–22: All of the recursive procedures shown so far have been directly recursive. That is, each procedure directly applied itself to a new argument. It is also possible to write two procedures that use each other, resulting in indirect recursion. Define the procedures **odd?** and **even?**, each in terms of the other. [*Hint:* What should each return when its argument is 0?]

Exercise 2–23: Use **map** to define a procedure, **transpose**, that takes a list of pairs and returns a pair of lists as follows:

(transpose '((a . 1) (b . 2) (c . 3)))   ⇒ ((a b c) 1 2 3)

(Remember, ((a b c) 1 2 3) is the same as ((a b c) . (1 2 3)).)

2-9 Assignment

Although most programs can be written without them, assignments to top-level definitions or let- and lambda-bound identifiers are sometimes useful. An assignment changes the value of the identifier, rather than creating a new binding, as with **let** or **lambda**. Assignments are performed with **set!**.

```
(define abcde '(a b c d e))
abcde                          ⇒ (a b c d e)
(set! abcde (cdr abcde))
abcde                          ⇒ (b c d e)
(let ([abcde '(a b c d e)])
    (set! abcde (reverse abcde))
    abcde)                     ⇒ (e d c b a)
```

Many languages require the use of an assignment to initialize local identifiers, separate from the declaration or binding of the identifier. In Scheme, all local identifiers are given a value immediately upon binding. Besides making the separate assignment to initialize local identifiers unnecessary, it ensures that the programmer cannot forget to initialize them, a common source of errors in most languages.

In fact, most of the assignments that are either necessary or convenient in other languages are both unnecessary and inconvenient in Scheme, since there is typically a clearer way to express the same algorithm without assignments. One common practice in some languages is to sequence expression evaluation with a sequence of assignments, as in the following procedure that finds the roots of a quadratic equation.

```
(define quadratic-formula
    (lambda (a b c)
        (let ([root1 0]
              [root2 0]
              [minusb 0]
              [radical 0]
              [divisor 0])
            (set! minusb (- 0 b))
            (set! radical (sqrt (- (* b b) (* 4 (* a c)))))
            (set! divisor (* 2 a))
            (set! root1 (/ (+ minusb radical) divisor))
            (set! root2 (/ (- minusb radical) divisor))
            (cons root1 root2))))
```

The roots are computed according to the well-known quadratic formula,

$$\frac{-b \pm \sqrt{b^2 - 4ac}}{2a},$$

which yields the solutions to the equation $0 = ax^2 + bx - c$. The let expression in this definition is employed solely to establish the identifier bindings, corresponding to the declarations required in other languages. The first three assignment expressions compute subpieces of the formula, namely $-b$, $\sqrt{b^2 - 4ac}$, and $2a$. The last two assignment expressions compute the two roots in terms of the subpieces. A pair of the two roots is the value of quadratic-formula. For example, the two roots of $2x^2 - 4x - 6$ are $x = 3$ and $x = -1$.

```
(quadratic-formula 2 -4 -6)   ⇒  (3 . -1)
```

The definition above works, but it can be written more clearly without the assignments.

```
(define quadratic-formula
    (lambda (a b c)
        (let ([minusb (- 0 b)]
              [radical (sqrt (- (* b b) (* 4 (* a c))))]
              [divisor (* 2 a)])
            (let ([root1 (/ (+ minusb radical) divisor)]
                  [root2 (/ (- minusb radical) divisor)])
                (cons root1 root2)))))
```

In this version, the set! expressions are gone, and we are left with essentially the same algorithm. However, by employing two let expressions, the definition makes clear the dependency of root1 and root2 on the values of minusb, radical, and divisor. Equally important, the let expressions make clear the *lack* of dependencies among minusb, radical, and divisor and between root1 and root2.

Assignments do have some uses in Scheme, otherwise the designers of Scheme would leave them out entirely. Consider the following modified cons that counts the number of times it is called, storing the count in an identifier named cons-count. It uses set! to increment the count; there is no way to achieve the same behavior without set! (or something similar).

```
(define cons-count 0)
(define cons
   (let ([old-cons cons])
      (lambda (x y)
         (set! cons-count (+ cons-count 1))
         (old-cons x y))))
```

```
(cons 'a '(b c))                      ⇒ (a b c)
cons-count                            ⇒ 1
(cons 'a (cons 'b (cons 'c '())))     ⇒ (a b c)
cons-count                            ⇒ 4
```

Assignments are commonly used to implement procedures that must maintain some internal state. For example, suppose we would like to define a procedure that returns 0 the first time it is called, 1 the second time, and so on indefinitely. We could write something similar to the definition of cons-count above:

```
(define next 0)
(define count
   (lambda ()
      (let ([v next])
         (set! next (+ next 1))
         v)))
```

```
(count)  ⇒ 0
(count)  ⇒ 1
```

This solution is undesirable because the identifier next is visible at top level even though it does not need to be. Since it is visible at top level, any code in the system can change its value, inadvertently affecting the behavior of count in a subtle way. We can solve this problem by binding next lexically outside of the lambda expression:

```
(define count
    (let ([next 0])
        (lambda ()
            (let ([v next])
                (set! next (+ next 1))
                v))))
```

The latter solution also generalizes easily to provide multiple counters, each with its own local counter. The procedure make-counter, defined below, returns a new counting procedure each time it is called.

```
(define make-counter
    (lambda ()
        (let ([next 0])
            (lambda ()
                (let ([v next])
                    (set! next (+ next 1))
                    v)))))
```

Since next is bound inside of make-counter but outside of the procedure returned by make-counter, each procedure it returns maintains its own unique counter.

```
(define count1 (make-counter))
(define count2 (make-counter))
(count1)                            ⇒ 0
(count2)                            ⇒ 0
(count1)                            ⇒ 1
(count1)                            ⇒ 2
(count2)                            ⇒ 1
```

As a more complex example using set!, let's consider the implementation of stack objects whose internal workings are not visible on the outside. Our stack objects should accept four *messages*: empty?, which returns #t if the stack is empty, push!, which adds an object to the top of the stack, top, which returns the object on the top of the stack, and pop!, which removes the

object on top of the stack. The procedure make-stack given below creates a
new stack each time it is called in a manner similar to make-counter.

```
(define make-stack
  (lambda ()
    (let ([ls '()])
      (lambda (msg . args)
        (cond
          [(eq? msg 'empty?) (null? ls)]
          [(eq? msg 'push!)
           (set! ls (cons (car args) ls))]
          [(eq? msg 'top) (car ls)]
          [(eq? msg 'pop!)
           (set! ls (cdr ls))])))))
```

Each stack is stored as a list bound to the identifier ls; set! is used to
change this binding by push! and pop!. Notice that the argument list of
the inside lambda expression uses the improper list syntax to bind args to a
list of all arguments but the first. This is useful here because in the case of
empty?, top, and pop! there is only one argument (the message), but in the
case of push! there are two (the message and the object to push onto the
stack).

```
(define stack1 (make-stack))
(define stack2 (make-stack))

(stack1 'empty?)                    ⇒ #t
(stack2 'empty?)                    ⇒ #t

(stack1 'push! 'a)
(stack1 'empty?)                    ⇒ #f
(stack2 'empty?)                    ⇒ #t

(stack1 'push! 'b)
(stack2 'push! 'c)
(stack1 'top)                       ⇒ b
(stack2 'top)                       ⇒ c

(stack1 'pop!)
(stack2 'empty?)                    ⇒ #f
(stack1 'top)                       ⇒ a

(stack2 'pop!)
(stack2 'empty?)                    ⇒ #t
```

As with the counters created by `make-counter`, the state maintained by each stack object is accessible only within the object. Each reference or change to this state is made explicitly by the object itself. One important benefit is that we can change the internal structure of the stack, perhaps using a vector instead of a list to hold the elements, without changing its external behavior. Because the behavior of the object is known abstractly (not operationally), it is known as an *abstract object*. See Section 9-5 for more about creating abstract objects.

Exercise 2-24: Modify `make-counter` to take two arguments: an initial value for the counter to use in place of 0, and an amount to increment the counter by each time.

Exercise 2-25: Modify the `stack` object to allow the two messages `ref` and `set!`. (*stack* 'ref *i*) would return the *i*th element from the top of the stack; (*stack* 'ref 0) would be equivalent to (*stack* 'top). Similarly, (*stack* 'set! *i* *v*) would change the *i*th element from the top of the stack to *v*. [*Hint:* Use `list-ref` to implement `ref`, and `list-tail` with `set-car!` to implement `set!`.]

2-10 Syntax

As we saw in Section 2-5, the `let` syntactic form is merely a *syntactic extension* defined in terms of a `lambda` expression and a procedure application, both core syntactic forms. At this point, you might be wondering which syntactic forms are core forms and which are syntactic extensions, and how syntactic extensions are defined. This section provides some answers to both questions.

The core syntactic forms are constants, identifiers, procedure applications, `quote` expressions, `lambda` expressions, `if` expressions, `set!` expressions, and `begin` expressions.

The only core form we we have not seen is `begin`. A `begin` expression has the form (begin exp_1 exp_2 ...). `begin` causes the expressions exp_1 exp_2 ... to be evaluated in sequence from left to right and returns the value of the last expression. It is typically used to sequence operations that perform side effects, such as `set!`.

```
(let ([x 3])
  (begin
    (set! x 'a)
    (cons x x)))  ⇒  (a . a)
```

The bodies of `lambda`, `let`, and `let*` expressions are implicitly `begin` expressions, since the expressions that make up the body are evaluated in a similar fashion, so the `let` expression above could be written without `begin`:

```
(let ([x 3])
  (set! x 'a)
  (cons x x))  ⇒  (a . a)
```

We took advantage of `let`'s implicit `begin` in Section 2–9 to perform `set!` expressions in a particular order.

The following grammar summarizes the core syntactic forms.

⟨core⟩	⟶	⟨constant⟩
	|	⟨identifier⟩
	|	(`quote` ⟨object⟩)
	|	(`lambda` ⟨parameters⟩ ⟨core⟩ ⟨core⟩ ...)
	|	(`if` ⟨core⟩ ⟨core⟩ ⟨core⟩)
	|	(`set!` ⟨identifier⟩ ⟨core⟩)
	|	(`begin` ⟨core⟩ ⟨core⟩ ...)
	|	(⟨core⟩ ⟨core⟩ ...)
⟨constant⟩	⟶	⟨boolean⟩
	|	⟨number⟩
	|	⟨character⟩
	|	⟨string⟩
⟨parameters⟩	⟶	⟨identifier⟩
	|	(⟨identifier⟩ ...)
	|	(⟨identifier⟩ ⟨identifier⟩ ... . ⟨identifier⟩)

⟨identifier⟩ is any Scheme identifier (symbol), ⟨object⟩ is any Scheme object such as a number, list, or symbol, ⟨boolean⟩ is either `#t` or `#f`, ⟨number⟩ is any number, ⟨character⟩ is any character, and ⟨string⟩ is any string. We have already seen examples of numbers, strings, lists, symbols, and booleans. See Chapter 5 for more on the object-level syntax of these and other objects.

There is one ambiguity in the grammar. The syntax for procedure applications, (⟨core⟩ ⟨core⟩ ...), is in conflict with the syntax for `quote`, `lambda`, if, set!, and begin expressions. In order to qualify as a procedure application, the first ⟨core⟩ must not be one of these keywords.

Now that we know exactly which syntactic forms are core syntactic forms, let's turn to a discussion of syntactic extensions. Syntactic extensions are so called because they extend the syntax of Scheme beyond the core syntax. There is virtually no restriction on what a syntactic extension can look like. However, all syntactic extensions in a Scheme expression must be expanded into core syntactic forms before evaluation takes place. This expansion is nearly always performed by a set of Scheme procedures, each capable of transforming one syntactic extension into a simpler form. This simpler form often contains other syntactic extensions, but this is no problem as long as these other syntactic extensions can be expanded into core syntactic forms.

You need never be conscious of the expansion process; the Scheme system automatically expands syntactic extensions prior to evaluation. In *Chez* Scheme, expansion may also be performed directly by invoking the procedure expand on a source expression.

```
(expand '(let ([x 3]) (+ x x)))  ⇒ ((lambda (x) (+ x x)) 3)
```

If you were to write your own evaluator for Scheme (see the interpreter example in Section 9–3), you might wish to take advantage of expand to reduce source expressions to the core syntactic forms.

There is no standard mechanism for defining syntactic extensions in Scheme. The mechanism employed in *Chez* Scheme and in this book was developed by Eugene Kohlbecker [11]. It is easier to learn and to use than traditional syntactic extension mechanisms and is likely to be adopted for use in many Scheme systems. The remainder of this section shows how to define the let syntactic extension; other examples appear in subsequent chapters. Syntactic extensions are defined with extend-syntax. extend-syntax is similar to define, except that it associates an automatically generated syntactic transformation procedure with a syntax keyword (such as let), rather than associating a top-level value with an identifier.

The easiest way to learn extend-syntax is to consider an example. Here is how we might define let with extend-syntax:

```
(extend-syntax (let)
  [(let ([x v] ...) e1 e2 ...)
   ((lambda (x ...) e1 e2 ...) v ...)])
```

The first subexpression appearing after extend-syntax is a list of keywords that may appear in the syntactic extension; the first element of this list is always the name of the syntactic form, *e.g.*, let or cond. In this case, the only keyword is let. For a cond expression, we would also include the keyword else (see the definition of cond in Section 8–1).

After the list of keywords comes a sequence of *pattern/expansion* pairs. Only one pattern/expansion pair appears in our definition for let. The *pattern* specifies what the input should look like and the *expansion* specifies what the output should look like. The pattern should always be a list whose first element is the principal syntax keyword, *i.e.*, the name of the syntactic form. If there is more than one pattern-expansion pair, the appropriate one is chosen by matching the patterns, in order, against the input during expansion. An error is signaled if none of the patterns match the input.

The notation *pat* ... in the pattern allows for zero or more expressions matching the ellipsis prototype *pat* in the input. Similarly, the notation *exp* ... in the expansion produces zero or more expressions from the ellipsis prototype *exp* in the output. The number of *pats* in the input determines the number of *exps* in the output; in order for this to work, any ellipsis prototype in the expansion must contain at least one pattern variable from an ellipsis prototype in the pattern.

The pattern/expansion pair in our definition for let should be fairly self-explanatory, but there are a few points worth mentioning. First, the syntax of let requires that there be at least one expression in the body, hence we have specified e1 e2 ... instead of e ..., which might seem more natural. On the other hand, let does not require that there be at least one identifier/value pair, so we were able to use, simply, [x v] .... Second, the pattern variables x and v, though together within the same prototype in the pattern, are separated in the expansion; any sort of rearrangement or recombination is possible. Finally, the three pattern variables x, v, and e2 that appear in ellipsis prototypes in the pattern also appear in ellipsis prototypes in the expansion. This is not a coincidence; it is a requirement. In general, if a pattern variable appears within an ellipsis prototype in the pattern, it cannot appear outside an ellipsis prototype in the expansion.

See Chapter 8 for a complete description of the extend-syntax and some substantial examples of its use.

Chapter 3: Binding Forms

This chapter describes the small set of syntactic forms whose primary purpose is to bind or assign identifiers. Other forms that bind or assign identifiers for which the binding or assignment is not the primary purpose (such as do) are found in later chapters, especially in Chapter 4. This chapter begins with the lambda syntactic form. All binding operations in Scheme are derived from lambda, except top-level occurrences of define, which establishes top-level bindings, or definitions, and extend-syntax, which establishes syntactic extensions associated with syntactic keywords.

3-1 Lambda

(lambda *idspec* *exp$_1$* *exp$_2$* ...)   syntax

    returns: a procedure

The lambda syntactic form is used to create procedures. Any operation that creates a procedure or local binding is ultimately defined in terms of lambda.

The identifiers in *idspec* are the formal parameters of the procedure, while the sequence of expressions *exp$_1$* *exp$_2$* ... is its body.

The body may begin with a sequence of definitions, in which case the definitions created are not top-level definitions but are instead local to the procedure. If definitions are present, the body is replaced by a letrec expression formed from the definitions and the remaining expressions. Consult Section 3–3 for more details. The remainder of this discussion on lambda assumes that this transformation has taken place, if necessary, so that the body is a sequence of expressions without definitions.

When the procedure is created, the bindings of all identifiers occurring free within the body, excluding the formal parameters, are retained with the procedure. Subsequently, whenever the procedure is applied to a list of actual parameters, the formal parameters are bound to the actual parameters, the retained bindings are restored, and the body is evaluated.

Upon application, the formal parameters defined by *idspec* are bound to the actual parameters as follows.

- If *idspec* is a proper list of identifiers, *e.g.*, (x y z), each identifier is bound to the corresponding actual parameter. An error is signaled if too few or too many actual parameters are supplied.

- If *idspec* is a single identifier (not in a list), *e.g.*, z, it is bound to a list of the actual parameters.

- If *idspec* is an improper list of identifiers terminated by an identifier, *e.g.*, (x y . z), each identifier but the last is bound to the corresponding actual parameter. The last identifier is bound to a list of the remaining actual parameters.

When the body is evaluated, the expressions exp_1 exp_2 ... are evaluated in sequence. The value of the last expression is the value of the procedure.

Procedures do not have a printed representation in the usual sense; there is no way to enter one from the keyboard or load one from a file without using lambda or another syntactic form that creates procedures. Scheme systems print procedures in different ways; this book uses the notation #<procedure>.

```
(lambda (x) (+ x 3))                ⇒ #<procedure>
((lambda (x) (+ x 3)) 7)            ⇒ 10
((lambda (x y) (* x (+ x y))) 7 13) ⇒ 140
((lambda (f x) (f x x)) + 11)       ⇒ 22
((lambda () (+ 3 4)))               ⇒ 7
((lambda (x . y) (list x y))
   28 37)                           ⇒ (28 (37))
((lambda (x . y) (list x y))
   28 37 47 28)                     ⇒ (28 (37 47 28))
((lambda (x y . z) (list x y z))
   1 2 3 4)                         ⇒ (1 2 (3 4))
((lambda x x) 7 13)                 ⇒ (7 13)
```

3-2 Local Binding

(let ((*id val*) ...) *exp*$_1$ *exp*$_2$ ...)   syntax

returns: the value of the final expression

The syntactic form `let` establishes local identifier bindings. Each identifier *id* is bound to the value of the corresponding expression *val*. The body of the `let`, in which the identifiers are bound, is the sequence of expressions *exp*$_1$ *exp*$_2$ ....

The forms `let`, `let*`, and `letrec` (`let*` and `letrec` are described after `let`) are similar but serve slightly different purposes. In contrast with `let*` and `letrec`, the expressions *val* ... are all outside the scope of the identifiers *id* .... Also, in contrast with `let*`, no ordering is implied for the evaluation of the expressions *val* .... They may be evaluated from left to right, from right to left, or in any other order at the discretion of the implementation. Use `let` whenever the values are independent of the identifiers and the order of evaluation is unimportant.

The body of a `let` expression may begin with a sequence of definitions, which establish bindings local to the body of the `let`. See the discussion of definitions under `lambda` in the preceding section or the more detailed explanation of local definitions found in Section 3–3.

The following `extend-syntax` definition for `let` shows the typical derivation of `let` from `lambda`.

```
(extend-syntax (let)
  [(let ([x v] ...) e1 e2 ...)
   ((lambda (x ...) e1 e2 ...) v ...)])
```

```
(let ([x (* 3.0 3.0)] [y (* 4.0 4.0)])
  (sqrt (+ x y)))                          ⇒ 5.0
(let ([x 'a] [y '(b c)])
  (cons x y))                              ⇒ (a b c)
(let ([x 0] [y 1])
  (let ([x y] [y x])
    (list x y)))                           ⇒ (1 0)
```

(let* ((id val) ...) exp_1 exp_2 ...)   syntax

    returns: the value of the final expression

The syntactic form let* is similar to let except that the expressions *val* ... are evaluated in sequence from left to right. Each of these expressions is within the scope of the identifiers to the left. Use let* when there is a linear dependency among the values, or when the order of evaluation is important.

Any let* expression may be converted to a set of nested let expressions. The following extend-syntax definition of let* demonstrates the typical transformation.

```
(extend-syntax (let*)
  [(let* () e1 e2 ...)
   (begin e1 e2 ...)]
  [(let* ([x1 v1] [x2 v2] ...) e1 e2 ...)
   (let ([x1 v1])
     (let* ([x2 v2] ...) e1 e2 ...))])
```

```
(let* ([x (* 5.0 5.0)]
       [y (- x (* 4.0 4.0))])
  (sqrt y))                    ⇒ 3.0
(let ([x 0] [y 1])
  (let* ([x y] [y x])
    (list x y)))               ⇒ (1 1)
```

(letrec ((id val) ...) exp_1 exp_2 ...)   syntax

    returns: the value of the final expression

The syntactic form letrec is similar to let and let*, except that it allows the definition of mutually recursive objects. Typically, the expressions *val* ... are lambda expressions and letrec is used to create mutually recursive procedures.

The order of evaluation of the expressions *val* ... is unspecified, and so it is an error to reference any of the identifiers bound by the letrec expression before all of the values have been computed. (Occurrence of an identifier within a lambda expression does not count as a reference, unless the resulting procedure is applied before all the values have been computed.)

Choose `letrec` over `let` or `let*` when there is a circular dependency among the identifiers and their values, and when the order of evaluation is unimportant.

One possible definition of `letrec` in terms of `let` and `set!` is given below.

```
(extend-syntax (letrec)
  [(letrec ([x v] ...) e1 e2 ...)
   (let ([x #f] ...)
     (set! x v) ...
     e1 e2 ...)])
```

The `let` expression establishes the identifier bindings. The initial value given each identifier is unimportant, so any value would do in place of `#f`. The bindings are established first so that the values may contain occurrences of the identifiers, *i.e.*, so that the values are computed within the scope of the identifiers. The `set!` expressions are used to assign each value to the appropriate identifier.

This is only one of many possible implementations of `letrec`. Two features of this implementation are worthy of note. First, this implementation evaluates the value expressions from left to right, which need not be true of other implementations. Second, it does not enforce the restriction that the values must not directly reference one of the identifiers; other implementations are free to do so.

```
(letrec ([sum
           (lambda (x)
             (if (zero? x)
                 0
                 (+ x (sum (1- x)))))])
  (sum 5))                                      ⇒ 15

(letrec ([even?
           (lambda (x)
             (or (zero? x)
                 (odd? (1- x))))]
         [odd?
           (lambda (x)
             (and (not (zero? x))
                  (even? (1- x))))])
  (even? 20))                                   ⇒ #t
```

(rec *id exp*)   syntax

returns: value of *exp*

The syntactic form rec creates a recursive object from *exp* by establishing
a binding of *id* within *exp* to the value of *exp*. In essence, it is a special
case of letrec for self-recursive objects.

This form is useful for creating recursive objects (especially procedures)
that do not depend on external identifiers for the recursion, which are
sometimes undesirable because the external bindings can change. For
example, a recursive procedure defined at top level depends on the value
of the top-level identifier given as its name. If the value of this identifier
should change, the meaning of the procedure itself would change. If the
procedure is defined instead with rec, its meaning is independent of the
identifier to which it is bound.

The two definitions below show rec first in terms of letrec, then in
terms of let and set!.

```
(extend-syntax (rec)
  [(rec x v)
   (letrec ([x v]) x)])
```

```
(extend-syntax (rec)
  [(rec x v)
   (let ([x v])
     (set! x v)
     x)])
```

The first form is simpler in appearance, but the second form is actually identical, as you can see by expanding the letrec in the first form
according to the transformation given earlier.

```
(map (rec sum
       (lambda (x)
         (if (= x 0)
             x
             (+ x (sum (- x 1)))))))
     '(0 1 2 3 4))                        ⇒ (0 1 3 6 10)
```

```
(define cycle
   (rec self
      (list (lambda () self))))
(eq? ((car cycle)) cycle)              ⇒ #t
```

3-3 Definitions

(define *id exp*)   syntax

(define (*id . idspec*) *exp₁ exp₂* ...)   syntax

> returns: unspecified

In the first form, define creates a new binding of *id* to the value of *exp*. The second form is a convenient shorthand for binding identifiers to procedures; it is identical to the following definition in terms of lambda:

```
(define id
   (lambda idspec
      exp₁ exp₂ ...))
```

Definitions normally appear at "top level," *i.e.*, outside the scope of any lambda or any form derived from lambda such as let, let*, or letrec. An identifier bound at top level is visible within any expression typed at the keyboard or loaded from a file, except where shadowed by a local binding and provided the reference does not occur before the definition.

Definitions may also appear at the front of a lambda body or body of any form derived from lambda. These *internal definitions* must precede the expressions in the body. Any lambda expression whose body begins with definitions may be transformed into an equivalent lambda expression without such definitions, by rewriting the body as a letrec expression. That is, a lambda expression of the form

```
(lambda idspec
   (define id val) ...
   exp₁ exp₂ ...)
```

may be expressed in the equivalent form

```
(lambda idspec
   (letrec ([id val] ...)
      exp₁ exp₂ ...))
```

Although this shows the transformation for the first and simpler form of definition, either form may appear within a lambda body.

```
(define x 3)
x                                    ⇒ 3
(define f
   (lambda (x y)
      (* (+ x y) 2)))
(f 5 4)                              ⇒ 18
(define (sum-of-squares x y)
   (+ (* x x) (* y y)))
(sum-of-squares 3 4)                 ⇒ 25
(define f
   (lambda (x)
      (+ x 1)))
(let ([x 2])
   (define f
      (lambda (y)
         (+ y x)))
   (f 3))                            ⇒ 5
(f 3)                                ⇒ 4
```

3-4 Assignment

(set! id exp)   syntax

   returns: unspecified

The syntactic form set! assigns a new value to an existing identifier. The value of the identifier id is changed to the value of exp. Any subsequent reference to id will evaluate to the new value.

This form is different from the forms described earlier in this chapter, because it does not establish a new binding for *id* but rather changes the value of an existing binding. Before the assignment, the identifier must be bound at top level, or it must be bound locally by an enclosing `lambda` expression or by some other binding form.

Assignments are not employed as frequently in Scheme as in most traditional languages, but they are useful for updating the state of a system and in creating recursive structures (as with `letrec`).

```
(let ((x 3) (y 4))
   (set! x 5)
   (+ x y))          ⇒ 9
(define f
   (lambda (x y)
      (cons x y)))
(f 'a 'b)            ⇒ (a . b)
(set! f
   (lambda (x y)
      (cons y x)))
(f 'a 'b)            ⇒ (b . a)
```

3-5 Fluid Binding

(fluid-let ((*id val*) ...) *exp₁* *exp₂* ...)   syntax

returns: value of the last expression

The syntactic form `fluid-let` provides a way to temporarily assign values to a set of identifiers. The new values are in effect only during the evaluation of the expression in the body of the `fluid-let` expression. The scopes of the identifiers are not determined by `fluid-let`; as with `set!`, the identifiers must be bound at top level or by an enclosing `lambda` or other binding form. It is possible, therefore, to control the scope of an identifier with `lambda` or `let` while establishing a new value with `fluid-let`.

Although it is similar in appearance to let, its operation is more like that of set!. Each *id* is assigned, as with set!, to the value of the corresponding *val* within the body *exp*$_1$ *exp*$_2$ .... Should the body exit normally or by invoking a continuation made outside of the body (see call/cc), the values in effect before the bindings were changed are restored. Should control return back to the body by the invocation of a continuation created within the body, the bindings are changed once again to the values in effect when the body last exited.

Fluid bindings are similar to *special* bindings in Lisp, except that (1) there is a single namespace for both lexical and fluid bindings, and (2) the scope of a fluidly bound identifier is not necessarily global. As with special bindings in Lisp, fluid bindings are most useful for maintaining identifiers that must be shared by a group of procedures. Upon entry to the group of procedures, the shared identifiers are fluidly bound to a new set of initial values so that on exit the original values are restored automatically. In this way, the group of procedures itself can be reentrant; it may call itself directly or indirectly without affecting the values of its shared identifiers.

```
(let ([x 3])
  (+ (fluid-let ([x 5])
       x)
     x))                            ⇒ 8
(let ([x 'a])
  (letrec ([f (lambda (y) (cons x y))])
    (fluid-let ([x 'b])
      (f 'c))))                     ⇒ (b . c)
(let ([x 'a])
  (call/cc
    (lambda (k)
      (letrec ([f (lambda (y) (k '*))])
        (f '*))))
  x)                                ⇒ a
```

Chapter 4: Control Operations

This chapter introduces the syntactic forms and procedures that serve as control structures for Scheme programs. Most control structures are syntactic forms rather than procedures, since they require special syntax.

4-1 Procedure Application

(procedure exp ...)   syntax

> returns: result of applying the value of *procedure* to the values of *exp ...*

Procedure application is the most basic Scheme control structure. Any list expression without a syntax keyword in the first position is a procedure application. The expressions *procedure* and *exp ...* are evaluated and the value of *procedure* is applied to the values of *exp ....*

The order in which the procedure and argument expressions are evaluated is unspecified. It may be left to right, right to left, or in some arbitrary order. However, the evaluation is guaranteed to be sequential; whatever order is chosen, each expression will be fully evaluated before evaluation of the next is started.

```
(+ 3 4)                          ⇒ 7
((if (odd? 3) + -) 6 2)          ⇒ 8
((lambda (x) x) 5)               ⇒ 5
(let ([f (lambda (x) (+ x x))])
    (f 8))                       ⇒ 16
```

(apply *procedure obj ... list*)   procedure

> returns: the result of applying *procedure* to *obj ...* and the elements of *list*

apply passes the first *obj* as the first argument to *procedure*, the second *obj* as the second argument, and so on for each object in *obj ...*, and passes the elements of *list* in order as the remaining arguments to *procedure*. Thus, *procedure* is called with as many arguments as there are *obj*s plus elements of *list*.

apply is useful when some or all of the arguments to be passed to a procedure are in a list, since it frees the programmer from explicitly destructuring the list.

```
(apply + '(4 5))                    ⇒ 9
(apply min '(6 8 3 2 5))            ⇒ 2
(apply min 5 1 3 '(6 8 3 2 5))      ⇒ 1
(apply vector 'a 'b '(c d e))       ⇒ #5(a b c d e)
(define first
   (lambda (l)
      (apply (lambda (x . y) x)
             l)))
(define rest
   (lambda (l)
      (apply (lambda (x . y) y)
             l)))
(first '(a b c d))                  ⇒ a
(rest '(a b c d))                   ⇒ (b c d)
```

4-2 Quoting

(quote *obj*)   syntax

    returns: *obj*

quote inhibits the normal evaluation rule for *obj*, allowing *obj* to be employed as data. Although any Scheme object may be quoted, quote is not necessary for constants, such as numbers, characters, and strings.

The expression (quote *exp*) may be abbreviated as '*exp*. The system reader (read) expands a single quote followed by an object into a quote expression.

```
(+ 2 3)           ⇒ 5
'(+ 2 3)          ⇒ (+ 2 3)
(quote (+ 2 3))   ⇒ (+ 2 3)
'a                ⇒ a
'cons             ⇒ cons
'()               ⇒ ()
```

'7   ⇒ 7

(quasiquote *obj*)   syntax

(unquote *obj*)   syntax

(unquote-splicing *obj*)   syntax

  returns: see explanation

  The expression (quasiquote *obj*) may be written as '*obj*, (unquote *obj*) as ,*obj*, and (unquote-splicing *obj*) as ,**@***obj*. The backward quote ('), comma (,), and comma-atsign (,**@**)are expanded by the procedure read into the corresponding syntactic form.

  unquote and unquote-splicing are only valid within quasiquote expressions.

  quasiquote is similar to quote, but it allows parts of the quoted text to be "unquoted."

  Within the quasiquote expression, any unquote form is evaluated. Any unquote-splicing form is evaluated, with the result spliced into the list structure. Any other form is left unevaluated.

  quasiquote expressions may be nested, with each quasiquote introducing a new level of quotation, and each unquote or unquote-splicing taking away a level of quotation. An expression nested within n quasiquote expressions must be within n unquote or unquote-splicing expressions to be evaluated.

```
'(+ 2 3)                     ⇒ (+ 2 3)
'(+ 2 ,(* 3 4))              ⇒ (+ 2 12)
'(a b (,(+ 2 3) c) d)        ⇒ (a b (5 c) d)
'(a b ,(reverse '(c d e)) f g)  ⇒ (a b (e d c) f g)
'(+ ,@(cdr '(* 2 3)))        ⇒ (+ 2 3)
'(a b ,@(reverse '(c d e)) f g)  ⇒ (a b e d c f g)
'',(cons 'a 'b)              ⇒ ',(cons 'a 'b)
'',(cons 'a 'b)              ⇒ '(a . b)
```

4-3 Sequencing

(begin exp_1 exp_2 ...)   syntax

    returns: the result of the last expression

The expressions exp_1 exp_2 ... are evaluated in sequence from left to
right. begin is used to sequence assignments, input/output, or other
operations that cause side effects.

The bodies of many syntactic forms, including lambda, let, let*, and
letrec, as well as the result clauses of cond, case and record-case, and
do, are treated as if they were inside an implicit begin; that is, the expressions making up the body or result clause are executed in sequence.
See the swap-pair! example below.

```
(define x 3)
(begin
  (set! x (+ x 1))
  (+ x x))          ⇒ 8

(define swap-pair!
  (lambda (x)
    (let ([temp (car x)])
      (set-car! x (cdr x))
      (set-cdr! x temp)
      x)))
(swap-pair! (cons 'a 'b))      ⇒ (b . a)
```

4-4 Conditionals

(if *test-exp then-exp else-exp*)   syntax

(if *test-exp then-exp*)   syntax

    returns: value of *then-exp* or *else-exp* depending on value of *else-exp*

If no *else-exp* is supplied and *test-exp* evaluates to a false value, the
result is unspecified. Usually, one of the syntactic forms when or unless
is preferable to an if expression without *else-exp*.

```
(let ([l '(a b c)])
  (if (null? l)
      '()
      (cdr l)))                    ⇒ (b c)
(let ([l '()])
  (if (null? l)
      '()
      (cdr l)))                    ⇒ ()
(let ([abs
       (lambda (x)
         (if (< x 0)
             (- 0 x)
             x))])
  (abs -4))                        ⇒ 4
(let ([x -4])
  (if (< x 0)
      (list 'minus (- 0 x))
      (list 'plus 4)))             ⇒ (minus 4)
```

(when *test-exp* *exp*$_1$ *exp*$_2$ ...)   syntax

   returns: unspecified

If *test-exp* evaluates to a true value, the expressions *exp*$_1$ *exp*$_2$ ... are evaluated in sequence. If *test-exp* evaluates to a false value, none of the expressions are evaluated.

```
(let ([x -4] [sign 'plus])
  (when (< x 0)
    (set! x (- 0 x))
    (set! sign 'minus))
  (list sign x))                   ⇒ (minus 4)
```

(unless *test-exp* *exp*$_1$ *exp*$_2$ ...)   syntax

   returns: unspecified

If *test-exp* evaluates to a false value, the expressions *exp*$_1$ *exp*$_2$ ... are evaluated in sequence. If *test-exp* evaluates to a true value, none of the expressions are evaluated.

```
(define check-pair
  (lambda (x)
    (unless (pair? x)
      (error 'check-pair "~s is not a pair" x))
    x))


(check-pair '(a b c))  ⇒ (a b c)
```

(not *obj***)**   procedure

   returns: #t if *obj* is a false value, #f otherwise

```
(not #f)      ⇒ #t
(not #t)      ⇒ #f
(not '(a b))  ⇒ #f
(not '())     ⇒ #t
```

(and *exp* **...)**   syntax

   returns: see explanation

   and evaluates its arguments in sequence from left to right and stops
   immediately (without evaluating the remaining arguments) if any expression evaluates to a false value. The value of the last expression
   evaluated is returned.

```
(let ([x 3])
  (and (> x 2) (< x 4)))   ⇒ #t
(let ([x 5])
  (and (> x 2) (< x 4)))   ⇒ #f
(and '() '(a b) '(c d))    ⇒ #f
(and '(a b) '(c d) '(e f)) ⇒ (e f)
```

(or *exp* **...)**   syntax

   returns: see explanation

   or evaluates its arguments in sequence from left to right and stops immediately (without evaluating the remaining arguments) if any expression
   evaluates to a true value. The value of the last expression evaluated is
   returned.

```
(let ([x 3])
    (or (< x 2) (> x 4)))  ⇒ #f
(let ([x 5])
    (or (< x 2) (> x 4)))  ⇒ #t
(or '() '(a b) '(c d))     ⇒ (a b)
```

(cond (*test-exp exp* ...) ... (else *exp* ...))   syntax

(cond (*test-exp exp* ...) ...)   syntax

> returns: the result of the last expression of the first true clause

A true clause is one whose *test-exp* evaluates to a true value. If the else clause is present as in the first form of cond shown above, it is considered to be a true clause. If there is no else clause and no true clause, the result is unspecified.

The expressions *exp* ... of the first true clause, if any, are evaluated in sequence. If there are no expressions *exp* ... in the first true clause, the value of *test-exp* is returned.

```
(let ([x 0])
    (cond
        [(< x 0) (list 'minus (abs x))]
        [(> x 0) (list 'plus x)]
        [else (list 'zero x)]))       ⇒ (zero 0)
```

(case *val* (*key exp* ...) ... (else *exp* ...))   syntax

(case *val* (*key exp* ...) ...)   syntax

> returns: the result of the last *exp* of the matching clause, if any

Each *key* is either a single object or a list of objects (any *key* that is a nonempty list is assumed to be a list of objects). No object should appear in more than one *key*. A matching clause is one whose *key* is or contains the value of *val*, according to the predicate eqv?. If there is no matching clause, and an else clause is present as in the first form of case shown above, it is considered to be a matching clause. If there is no matching clause and no else clause, the result is unspecified.

The expressions *exp* ... of the matching clause, if any, are evaluated in sequence.

```
(let ([x 4] [y 5])
   (case (+ x y)
      [(1 3 5 7 9) 'odd]
      [(0 2 4 6 8) 'even]
      [else 'out-of-range]))   ⇒ odd
```

(record-case *val* (*key idspec exp* ...) ... (else *exp* ...))   syntax

(record-case *val* (*key idspec exp* ...) ...)   syntax

returns: the result of the last *exp* of the matching clause, if any

record-case is a restricted form of *case* that supports the destructuring of *records*, or *tagged lists*. A record has as its first element a tag that determines what "type" of record it is; the remaining elements are the fields of the record.

Each *key* is an object or list of objects, as with case, and no object should appear in more than one *key*. The selection of a matching clause is similar to that for case, except that *val* must be a pair, and the *keys* are compared against the car of that pair, rather than against the pair itself, again with eqv?.

Once a matching clause has been selected, the elements of the list are bound to the identifiers in *idspec* as in the application of a lambda expression (see Section 3–1). If the else clause is selected, no such binding is performed. The expressions *exp* ... of the matching clause are evaluated in sequence within the scope of the bound identifiers.

```
(define calc
   (lambda (x)
      (record-case x
         [add (x y) (+ x y)]
         [sub (x y) (- x y)]
         [mul (x y) (* x y)]
         [div (x y) (/ x y)]
         [else
          (error 'calc "invalid expression ~s" x)]))))

(calc '(add 3 4))   ⇒ 7
(calc '(div 3 4))   ⇒ 3/4
```

4-5 Recursion, Iteration, and Mapping

(let *name* ((*id val*) ...) *exp*$_1$ *exp*$_2$ ...)   syntax

returns: value of the last expression

This form of let, called *named let*, is a general-purpose iteration and recursion mechanism. It is similar to the more common form of let (see Section 3–2) in the binding of the identifiers *id* ... to the values *id* ... within the body *exp*$_1$ *exp*$_2$ .... In addition, the identifier *name* is bound within the body to a procedure that may be called to recur or iterate; the arguments to the procedure become the new values for the identifiers *id* ....

Just as unnamed let can be expressed as a simple direct application of a lambda expression to arguments, named let can be expressed as the application of a recursive procedure to arguments. A named let expression of the form

        (let *name* ([*id val*] ...)
          exp$_1$ *exp*$_2$ ...)

can be rewritten with letrec as

        (letrec ([*name* (lambda (*id* ...) *exp*$_1$ *exp*$_2$ ...)])
          (*name val* ...))

or with rec as

        ((rec *name* (lambda (*id* ...) *exp*$_1$ *exp*$_2$ ...))
          val ...).

Scheme guarantees to optimize tail recursion into loops, so tail recursion does not build up any sort of control stack that might be associated with normal (not tail) recursion. Tail recursion is a special form of recursion that can be recognized at the point of a recursive call. If the value of a procedure is the value of the recursive call, then the call is tail-recursive. If, on the other hand, some operation is performed on the result of the recursive call, the call is not tail-recursive. Because of this, recursion in general and named let in particular provide a natural way to implement many algorithms, whether iterative, recursive, or partly iterative and partly recursive; the programmer is not burdened with two distinct mechanisms.

The following two definitions of **factorial** use named **let** expressions to compute the factorial $n!$ of a nonnegative integer n. The first employs the standard recursive definition $n! = n \times (n - 1)!$ where $0!$ is defined to be 1. The second is an iterative version that employs the iterative definition $n! = n \times (n - 1) \times (n - 2) \times \ldots \times 1$, using an accumulator, a, to hold the intermediate products.

```
(define factorial
   (lambda (n)
      (let fact ([i n])
         (if (zero? i)
             1
             (* i (fact (- i 1)))))))
```

```
(factorial 0)    ⇒ 1
(factorial 1)    ⇒ 1
(factorial 2)    ⇒ 2
(factorial 3)    ⇒ 6
(factorial 10)   ⇒ 3628800
```

```
(define factorial
   (lambda (n)
      (let fact ([i n] [a 1])
         (if (zero? i)
             a
             (fact (- i 1) (* a i)))))))
```

A related problem is to compute the nth Fibonacci number for a given n. The *Fibonacci numbers* are an infinite sequence of integers, 0, 1, 1, 2, 3, 5, 8, *etc.*, where each number is the sum of the two previous numbers in the sequence [10]. A procedure to compute the nth Fibonacci number is most naturally defined recursively as follows:

```
(define fibonacci
   (lambda (n)
      (let fib ([i n])
         (cond
             [(= i 0) 0]
             [(= i 1) 1]
             [else (+ (fib (- i 1)) (fib (- i 2)))])))))
```

```
(fibonacci 0)    ⇒ 0
(fibonacci 1)    ⇒ 1
(fibonacci 2)    ⇒ 1
(fibonacci 3)    ⇒ 2
(fibonacci 4)    ⇒ 3
(fibonacci 5)    ⇒ 5
(fibonacci 6)    ⇒ 8
(fibonacci 20)   ⇒ 6765
```

However, this solution requires computation of the two previous Fibonacci numbers and hence is *doubly recursive*. For example, to compute (fibonacci 4) requires the computation of both (fib 3) and (fib 2), to compute (fib 3) requires computing both (fib 2) and (fib 1), and to compute (fib 2) requires computing both (fib 1) and (fib 0). This is very inefficient, and it becomes more inefficient as n grows. A more efficient solution is to adapt the accumulator solution of the factorial example above to use two accumulators, a1 for the current Fibonacci number and a2 for the previous.

```
(define fibonacci
    (lambda (n)
        (if (= n 0)
            0
            (let fib ([i n] [a1 1] [a2 0])
                (if (= i 1)
                    a1
                    (fib (- i 1) (+ a1 a2) a1)))))))
```

Here, zero is treated as a special case, since there is no previous value. This allows us to use the single base case (= i 1). The time it takes to compute the nth Fibonacci number using this iterative solution grows linearly with n, which makes a significant difference when compared to the doubly recursive version. To get a feel for the difference, try computing (fibonacci 20) using both definitions to see how long each takes.

The named let examples shown so far are either tail-recursive or not tail-recursive. It often happens that one recursive call within the same expression is tail recursive while another is not. The definition for factor below computes the prime factors of its nonnegative integer argument; the first call to f is not tail-recursive but the second one is.

```
(define factor
   (lambda (n)
      (let f ([n n] [i 2])
         (cond
            [(> i n) '()]
            [(integer? (/ n i))
             (cons i (f (/ n i) i))]
            [else
             (f n (+ i 1))]))))))

(factor 12)         ⇒ (2 2 3)
(factor 3628800)    ⇒ (2 2 2 2 2 2 2 3 3 3 3 5 5 7)
(factor 9239)       ⇒ (9239)
```

(map *procedure* *list*$_1$ *list*$_2$ ...)   procedure

returns: list of results

map applies *procedure* to corresponding elements of the lists *list*$_1$ *list*$_2$ ...
and returns a list of the resulting values. The lists *list*$_1$ *list*$_2$ ... must
be of the same length, and *procedure* must expect as many arguments as
there are lists.

While the order in which the applications themselves occur is not specified, the order of the values in the output list is the same as that of the
corresponding values in the input lists.

```
(map abs '(1 -2 3 -4 5 -6))  ⇒ (1 2 3 4 5 6)
(map (lambda (x y) (* x y))
    '(1 2 3 4)
    '(8 7 6 5))              ⇒ (8 14 18 20)
```

map might be defined as follows.

```
(define map
   (lambda (f ls . more)
      (if (null? more)
          (let map1 ([ls ls])
             (if (null? ls)
                 '()
                 (cons (f (car ls))
                       (map1 (cdr ls)))))
```

```
(let map-more ([ls ls] [more more])
  (if (or (null? ls) (ormap null? more))
      '()
      (cons (apply f
                   (car ls)
                   (map car more))
            (map-more (cdr ls)
                      (map cdr more)))))))))
```

One interesting feature of this definition is that map uses itself to pull out the cars and cdrs of the list of input lists; this works because of the special treatment of the single list argument case. Another is that the procedure apply takes care of passing the values in the list returned by (map car more) as arguments to f.

(for-each *procedure list₁ list₂ ...*)   procedure

returns: unspecified

for-each is similar to map except that for-each does not create and return a list of the resulting values, and for-each guarantees to perform the applications in sequence over the lists from left to right.

```
(let ([same-count 0])
  (for-each
    (lambda (x y)
      (when (= x y)
        (set! same-count (+ same-count 1))))
    '(1 2 3 4 5 6)
    '(2 3 3 4 7 6))
  same-count)                                         ⇒ 3
```

(ormap *procedure list₁ list₂ ...*)   procedure

returns: see explanation

ormap applies the procedure *procedure* to corresponding elements of the lists *list₁ list₂* ... in sequence until either the lists run out or *procedure* returns a true value. The value of the last application of *procedure* is returned. The lists *list₁ list₂* ... must be of the same length, and *procedure* must expect as many arguments as there are lists.

```
(ormap symbol? '(1.0 #\a "hi" '()))      ⇒ #f
(ormap member
       '(a b c)
       '((c b) (b a) (a c)))             ⇒ (b a)
(ormap (lambda (x y z) (= (+ x y) z))
       '(1 2 3 4)
       '(1.2 2.3 3.4 4.5)
       '(2.3 4.4 6.4 8.6))              ⇒ #t
```

(andmap *procedure* *list*$_1$ *list*$_2$ ...)   procedure

    returns: see explanation

andmap applies the procedure *procedure* to corresponding elements of the
lists *list*$_1$ *list*$_2$ ... in sequence until either the lists run out or *procedure*
returns a false value. The value of the last application of *procedure*
is returned. The lists *list*$_1$ *list*$_2$ ... must be of the same length, and
procedure must expect as many arguments as there are lists.

```
(andmap symbol? '(a b c d))            ⇒ #t
(andmap =
        '(1 2 3 4)
        '(1.0 2.0 3.0 4.0))            ⇒ #t
(andmap (lambda (x y z) (= (+ x y) z))
        '(1 2 3 4)
        '(1.2 2.3 3.4 4.5)
        '(2.2 4.3 6.5 8.5))            ⇒ #f
```

(do ((*id val update*) ...) (*test res* ...) *exp* ...)   syntax

    returns: the value of the last *res*

do performs a common restricted form of iteration. The set of identifiers
id ... are assigned the initial values *val* ... and given the new values
update ... on each subsequent iteration. After the bindings for the
identifiers have been established, the test expression *test* is evaluated.
If the value of *test* is a true value, iteration is discontinued and the
expressions *res* ... are evaluated in sequence, and the value of the last *res*
expression is returned. If the value of *test* is a false value, the expressions
exp ... are evaluated in sequence and iteration continues.

The expressions *exp* ... are evaluated only for effect and often are omitted entirely. The expressions *res* ... may be absent, in which case the value of the do expression is unspecified. Any *update* expression may be omitted, and the effect is the same as if the *update* were simply the corresponding *id*, i.e., (*id val id*).

The definitions for factorial and fibonacci below are straightforward translations of the tail-recursive definitions given under named let above. The definition of divisors is similar to the tail-recursive definition for factor given under named let; divisors computes the nontrivial divisors of a nonnegative integer. The use of do in divisors illustrates omitting an update and including an expression to evaluate for effect; however, it does not demonstrate good programming style. The computation of the new value for divisors should take place in the update expression for divisors, rather than in the body of the do.

```
(define factorial
   (lambda (n)
      (do ([i n (- i 1)] [a 1 (* a i)])
          ((zero? i) a))))
```

(factorial 10)   ⇒ 3628800

```
(define fibonacci
   (lambda (n)
      (if (= n 0)
          0
          (do ([i n (- i 1)] [a1 1 (+ a1 a2)] [a2 0 a1])
              ((= i 1) a1)))))
```

(fibonacci 6)   ⇒ 8

```
(define divisors
   (lambda (n)
      (do ([divisors '()] [i 2 (+ i 1)])
          ((>= i n) divisors)
          (when (integer? (/ n i))
             (set! divisors
                (cons i divisors))))))
```

```
(divisors 5)        ⇒ ()
(divisors 32)       ⇒ (16 8 4 2)
```

4-6 Continuations

During the evaluation of a Scheme expression, the system must know two things:

- what to evaluate, and
- what to do with the value.

Consider the evaluation of (null? x) within the expression

```
(if (null? x) (quote ()) (cdr x)).
```

The system must first evaluate (null? x) and, based on its value, evaluate either (quote ()) or (cdr x). "What to evaluate" is (null? x), and "what to do with the value" is to make the decision which of (quote ()) and (cdr x) to evaluate and do so. We call "what to do with the value" the *continuation* of a computation.

Thus, at any point during the evaluation of any expression, there is a continuation ready to complete, or at least *continue*, the computation from that point. Let's assume that x has the value (a b c). Then we can isolate six continuations during the evaluation of (if (null? x) (quote ()) (cdr x)), the continuations waiting for:

1. the value of (if (null? x) (quote ()) (cdr x)),
2. the value of (null? x),
3. the value of null?,
4. the value of x,
5. the value of cdr, and
6. the value of x (again).

The continuation of (cdr x) is not listed because it is the same as the one waiting for (if (null? x) (quote ()) (cdr x)).

Scheme allows these continuations to be obtained with call/cc.

```
(call-with-current-continuation procedure)                    procedure
(call/cc procedure)                                           procedure
```

returns: the result of applying *procedure* to the current continuation

call-with-current-continuation and call/cc are two names for the same procedure; the abbreviation call/cc is more often used, for the obvious reason that it requires fewer keystrokes to type.

call/cc obtains its continuation and passes it to *procedure*, which must expect one argument. The continuation itself is represented by a procedure of one argument. Each time this procedure is applied to a value, it returns the value to the continuation of the call/cc application. That is, when the continuation procedure is given a value, it returns the value as the result of the application of call/cc.

If *procedure* returns normally when passed the continuation procedure, the value returned by call/cc is the value returned by *procedure*.

In reality, a continuation may exist only conceptually, with no one data structure containing all of the information required to continue the computation. call/cc gathers all of the necessary information no matter how it is stored, and is thus a portable, high-level mechanism.

Continuations allow the implementation of nonlocal exits (from procedures or loops, for example), backtracking [19, 3], coroutines [5], multitasking [20], and engines (Section 9–7).

Consider the simple examples below.

```
(call/cc
  (lambda (k)
    (* 5 4)))              ⇒ 20
(call/cc
  (lambda (k)
    (* 5 (k 4))))         ⇒ 4
(+ 2
  (call/cc
    (lambda (k)
      (* 5 (k 4)))))      ⇒ 6
```

In the first example, the continuation is obtained and bound to k, but k is never used, so the value is simply the value of the multiplication 3 and 4. In the second, the continuation is invoked before the multiplication, so the value is the value passed to the continuation, 4. The third example shows that the value returned from call/cc can be used for further computation.

Here is a more practical example, showing the use of call/cc to provide a nonlocal exit from a loop.

```
(define member
   (lambda (x ls)
      (call/cc
         (lambda (break)
            (do ([ls ls (cdr ls)])
                ((null? ls) #f)
                (when (equal? x (car ls))
                   (break ls)))))))

(member 'd '(a b c))  ⇒ #f
(member 'b '(a b c))  ⇒ (b c)
```

The continuation invocations above are performed before call/cc returns. The following example uses the continuation after call/cc returns.

```
(let ([x (call/cc (lambda (k) k))])
   (x (lambda (ignore) "hi")))        ⇒ "hi"
```

The continuation obtained by this call to call/cc may be described as, "Take the value, bind it to x, and apply the value of x to the value of (lambda (ignore) "hi")." Since (lambda (k) k) returns its argument, x is bound to the continuation itself; this continuation is applied to the procedure resulting from the evaluation of (lambda (ignore) "hi"). This has the effect of binding x (again!) to this procedure and applying the procedure to itself. The procedure ignores its argument and returns "hi".

The following variation of the example above is probably the most confusing Scheme program of its size; nearly everyone guesses what it returns, but it takes some work to verify that guess.

```
(((call/cc (lambda (k) k)) (lambda (x) x)) 'HEY!)  ⇒ HEY!
```

The value of the call/cc is its own continuation, as in the previous example. This is applied to the identity procedure (lambda (x) x), so the call/cc returns a second time with this value. Then, the identity procedure is applied to itself, yielding the identity procedure. This is finally applied to 'HEY!, yielding HEY!.

Continuations used in this manner do not always cause this much confusion. Consider the following definition for factorial that saves the continuation at the base of the recursion before returning 1, by assigning the top-level identifier retry.

```
(define retry #f)
(define factorial
   (lambda (x)
      (if (= x 0)
          (call/cc (lambda (k) (set! retry k) 1))
          (* x (factorial (- x 1)))))))
```

Applying this definition factorial works as we expect factorial to work, except it has the side effect of assigning retry.

```
(factorial 4)  ⇒ 24
```

The continuation bound to retry might be described as, "Multiply the value by 1, then multiply this result by 2, then multiply this result by 3, then multiply this result by 4." If we pass the contination a different value, i.e., not 1, we will cause the base value to be something other than 1 and hence change the end result.

```
(retry 2)  ⇒ 48
```

```
(retry 5)  ⇒ 120
```

This mechanism could be the basis for a breakpoint package implemented with call/cc; each time a breakpoint is encountered, the continuation of the breakpoint is saved so that the computation may be restarted from the breakpoint (more than once, if desired).

See Section 9–7 for the implementation of engines with call/cc in co-operation with timer interrupts, and see the references given above for other uses for continuations.

(dynamic-wind *in body out*)   procedure

> returns: result of applying *body*

dynamic-wind offers "protection" from continuation invocation. It is useful for performing tasks that must be performed whenever control enters or leaves *body*, either normally or by continuation application.

The three arguments *in*, *body*, and *out* must be procedures of no arguments, *i.e.*, *thunks*. Before applying *body*, and each time *body* is entered subsequently by the application of a continuation created within *body*, the *in* thunk is applied. Upon normal exit from *body*, and each time *body* is exited by the application of a continuation created outside *body*, the *out* thunk is applied.

Thus, it is guaranteed that *in* is invoked at least once. In addition, if *body* ever returns, *out* is invoked at least once.

Most Lisp systems provide a similar facility (unwind-protect) for protection from nonlocal exits. This is often sufficient. However, unwind-protect only provides the equivalent to *out*, since most Lisp systems do not provide fully general continuations. Here is how unwind-protect might be specified with dynamic-wind:

```
(extend-syntax (unwind-protect)
  [(unwind-protect body cleanup ...)
   (dynamic-wind
       (lambda () #f)
       (lambda () body)
       (lambda () cleanup ...))])
```

The following example demonstrates the use of dynamic-wind to be sure that an input port is closed after processing, regardless of whether the processing completes normally.

```
(let ([p (open-input-file "input-file")])
  (dynamic-wind
      (lambda () #f)
      (lambda () (process p))
      (lambda () (close-input-port p))))
```

This example uses both *in* and *out* thunks to cause a pair of identifiers to be swapped before and after the evaluation of the *body*. Unfortunately, it does not show the effects of the application of continuations within and outside of the body; such an example would be too involved for this presentation. This same mechanism can be adapted to support fluid binding as provided by `fluid-let` [7].

```
(let ([x 'a] [y 'b])
   (let ([swap
          (lambda ()
             (let ([temp x])
                (set! x y)
                (set! y temp)))])                  ((a . b)
      (list (cons x y)                         ⇒  (b . a)
            (dynamic-wind                          (a . b))
               swap
               (lambda () (cons x y))
               swap)
            (cons x y))))
```

4-7 Engines

Engines are a high-level process abstraction supporting *timed preemption*, introduced in 1984 by Christopher T. Haynes and Daniel P. Friedman [6]. Engines may be used to simulate multiprocessing, implement operating system kernels, and perform nondeterministic computations.

An engine is created by passing a thunk (procedure of no arguments) to make-engine. The body of the thunk is the computation to be performed by the engine. An engine itself is a procedure of three arguments:

1 *ticks.* *ticks* is a positive integer that specifies the amount of *fuel* to be given to the engine. An engine executes until this fuel runs out or until its computation finishes.

2 *complete.* *complete* is a procedure of two arguments that specifies what to do if the computation finishes. Its arguments will be the result of the computation and the amount of fuel left over.

3 *expire.* *expire* is a procedure of one argument that specifies what to do if the fuel runs out before the computation finishes. Its argument will

be a new engine capable of continuing the computation from the point of interruption.

When an engine is applied to its arguments, it sets up a timer (see set-timer in Section 7–9 and the engine implementation in Section 9–7) to fire in *ticks* time units. If the engine computation completes before the timer goes off, the system invokes *complete*, passing it the value of the computation and the number of *ticks* left over. If, on the other hand, the timer goes off before the engine computation completes, the system creates a new engine from the continuation of the interrupted computation and passes this engine to *expire*. *complete* and *expire* return their value to the continuation of the engine invocation.

(make-engine *thunk*)   procedure

>   returns: an engine

Do not use the timer interrupt (see set-timer) and engines at the same time, since engines are implemented in terms of the timer (Section 9–7). The timer should be used directly only when low-level access to the interrupt facilities is required.

The following example creates an engine from a trivial computation, 3, and gives the engine 10 ticks.

```
(define eng
   (make-engine
      (lambda () 3)))
(eng 10
     (lambda (value ticks) value)
     (lambda (x) x))              ⇒ 3
```

It is often useful to pass cons as the *complete* procedure to an engine, causing the engine to return a pair of the value and the ticks remaining if the computation completes.

```
(define eng
   (make-engine
      (lambda () 3)))
(eng 10
     cons
     (lambda (x) x))    ⇒ (3 . 9)
```

In the example above, the value was 3 and there were 9 ticks left over, *i.e.*, it took only one unit of fuel to evaluate 3. (The fuel amounts given here are for illustration only. Your mileage may vary.)

Typically, the engine computation does not finish in one try. The following example displays the use of an engine to compute the 10th Fibonacci number (see Section 4–5) in steps.

```
(define fibonacci
   (lambda (n)
      (let fib ([i n])
         (cond
            [(= i 0) 0]
            [(= i 1) 1]
            [else (+ (fib (- i 1))
                     (fib (- i 2)))]))))
(define eng
   (make-engine
      (lambda ()
         (fibonacci 10))))

(eng 50
     cons
     (lambda (new-eng)
       (set! eng new-eng)
       "expired"))          ⇒ "expired"
(eng 50
     cons
     (lambda (new-eng)
       (set! eng new-eng)
       "expired"))          ⇒ "expired"
(eng 50
     cons
     (lambda (new-eng)
       (set! eng new-eng)
       "expired"))          ⇒ "expired"
(eng 50
     cons
     (lambda (new-eng)
       (set! eng new-eng)
```

```
"expired"))          ⇒ (55 . 21)
```

Each time the engine's fuel ran out, the *expire* procedure assigned eng to the new engine. The entire computation required four blocks of 50 ticks to complete; of the last 50 it used all but 21. Thus, the total amount of fuel used was 179 ticks. This leads us to the following procedure, mileage, which "times" a computation using engines:

```
(define mileage
    (lambda (thunk)
        (let loop ([eng (make-engine thunk)] [total-ticks 0])
            (eng 50
                (lambda (value ticks)
                    (+ total-ticks (- 50 ticks)))
                (lambda (new-eng)
                    (loop new-eng
                        (+ total-ticks 50)))))))
```

```
(mileage (lambda () (fibonacci 10)))   ⇒ 179
```

The choice of 50 for the number of ticks to use each time is arbitrary, of course. It might make more sense to pass a much larger number, say 10000, in order to reduce the number of times the computation is interrupted.

The next procedure is similar to mileage, but it returns a list of engines, one for each tick it takes to complete the computation. Each of the engines in the list represents a "snapshot" of the computation, analogous to a single frame of a moving picture. This procedure was defined and actually put to use by the Indiana University student Perry Wagle. snapshot might be useful for "single stepping" a computation.

```
(define snapshot
    (lambda (thunk)
        (let again ([eng (make-engine thunk)])
            (cons eng
                (eng 1 (lambda (v t) '()) again)))))
```

The recursion embedded in this procedure is rather strange. The complete procedure is the base case, returning the empty list, and the expire procedure is the recursion step.

The next procedure, round-robin, could be the basis for a simple time-sharing operating system. round-robin maintains a queue of processes (a list of engines), cycling through the queue in a *round-robin* fashion, allowing each process to run for a set amount of time. round-robin returns a list of the values returned by the engine computations in the order that the computations complete.

```
(define round-robin
  (lambda (engs)
    (if (null? engs)
        '()
        ((car engs)
         1
         (lambda (value ticks)
           (cons value (round-robin (cdr engs))))
         (lambda (eng)
           (round-robin
             (append (cdr engs) (list eng)))))))))
```

Since the amount of fuel passed in each time, one tick, is constant, the effect of round-robin is to return a list of the values sorted from the quickest to complete to the slowest to complete. Thus, when we call round-robin on a list of engines, each computing one of the Fibonacci numbers, the output list is sorted with the earlier Fibonacci numbers first, regardless of the order of the input list.

```
(round-robin
  (map (lambda (x)
         (make-engine
           (lambda ()
             (fibonacci x))))
       '(4 5 2 8 3 7 6 2)))        ⇒ (1 1 2 3 5 8 13 21)
```

More interesting things could happen if the amount of fuel varied each time through the loop. In this case, the computation would be nondeterministic, *i.e.*, the results would vary from call to call.

The following syntactic form, por (parallel-or), returns the first of its expressions to complete with a true value. por is implemented with the procedure first-true, which is similar to round-robin but quits when any of the engines completes with a true value. If all of the engines

complete, but none with a true value,   first-true (and hence por)
returns #f. Also, although first-true passes a fixed amount of fuel to
each engine, it chooses the next engine to run at random, and is thus
nondeterminsistic.

```
(extend-syntax (por)
  [(por x ...)
   (first-true
      (list (make-engine (lambda () x)) ...))])
(define first-true
  (let ([pick
           (lambda (ls)
              (list-ref ls (random (length ls))))])
     (lambda (engs)
        (if (null? engs)
            #f
            (let ([eng (pick engs)])
               (eng 1
                    (lambda (val ticks)
                       (or val
                           (first-true
                              (remq eng engs))))
                    (lambda (new-eng)
                       (first-true
                          (cons new-eng
                                (remq eng engs)))))))))))
```

The list of engines is maintained with pick, which randomly chooses
an element of the list, and remq, which removes the chosen engine from
the list. Since por is nondeterministic, subsequent uses with the same
expressions may not return the same values.

```
(por 1 2 3)  ⇒ 2
(por 1 2 3)  ⇒ 3
(por 1 2 3)  ⇒ 2
(por 1 2 3)  ⇒ 1
```

Furthermore, even if one of the expressions is an infinite loop, por can
still finish (as long as one of the other expressions completes and returns
a true value).

```
(por (let loop () (loop)) 2)   ⇒ 2
```

With `engine-return` and `engine-block`, it is possible to terminate an engine explicitly. `engine-return` causes the engine to complete, as if the computation had finished. Its argument is passed to the *complete* procedure along with the number of ticks remaining. It is essentially a nonlocal exit from the engine. Similarly, `engine-block` causes the engine to expire, as if the timer had run out. A new engine is made from the continuation of the call to `engine-block` and passed to the *expire* procedure.

(engine-block)   procedure

> returns: does not return

This causes a running engine to stop, create a new engine capable of continuing the computation, and pass it to its own third argument (the expire procedure). Any remaining fuel is forfeited.

```
(define eng
   (make-engine
      (lambda ()
         (engine-block)
         "completed")))

(eng 100
      (lambda (value ticks) value)
      (lambda (x)
         (set! eng x)
         "expired"))                ⇒ "expired"
(eng 100
      (lambda (value ticks) value)
      (lambda (x)
         (set! eng x)
         "expired"))                ⇒ "completed"
```

(engine-return *obj*)   procedure

> returns: does not return

This causes a running engine to stop and pass control to the second argument of the engine (the complete procedure). The first argument passed to the complete procedure is *obj*, and the second argument is the amount of fuel remaining, as usual.

```
(define eng
    (make-engine
        (lambda ()
            (cons (engine-return 'a) 'b))))

(eng 100
        (lambda (value ticks) value)
        (lambda (new-eng) "expired"))  ⇒ a
```

4-8 Delayed Evaluation

The syntactic form `delay` and the procedure `force` may be used in combination to implement *lazy evaluation*. An expression subject to lazy evaluation is not evaluated until its value is required, and once evaluated is never reevaluated.

(delay *exp*)   syntax

> returns: a promise

> A *promise* is similar to a procedure of no arguments that evaluates its body only once and returns the same value no matter how many times it is invoked. The first time a promise is *forced* (with `force`), it evaluates its body, "remembering" the resulting value. Thereafter, each time the promise is forced, it returns the remembered value instead of reevaluating its body.

> See the examples given for `force` below.

(force *promise*)   procedure

> returns: result of forcing *promise*

> `delay` and `force` may be implemented in terms of first-class procedures as follows.

```
(extend-syntax (delay)
  [(delay exp)
   (let ([thunk (lambda () exp)])
     (lambda ()
       (let ([v (thunk)])
         (set! thunk (lambda () v))
         v)))])
(define force
  (lambda (promise)
    (promise)))
```

delay and force are typically only used in the absence of side effects, *e.g.*, assignments, so that the order of evaluation is unimportant. The benefit to using delay and force is one of efficiency; some amount of computation might be avoided altogether if it is delayed until absolutely required.

```
(define stream-car
  (lambda (s)
    (car (force s))))
(define stream-cdr
  (lambda (s)
    (cdr (force s))))
(define counters
  (let next ([n 1])
    (delay (cons n (next (+ n 1))))))

(stream-car counters)                 ⇒ 1
(stream-car (stream-cdr counters))    ⇒ 2

(define stream-add
  (lambda (s1 s2)
    (delay
      (cons
        (+ (stream-car s1) (stream-car s2))
        (stream-add (stream-cdr s1) (stream-cdr s2))))))
(define even-counters
  (stream-add counters counters))
```

```
(stream-car even-counters)                ⇒ 2
(stream-car (stream-cdr even-counters))   ⇒ 4
```

Chapter 5: Operations on Objects

This chapter describes the operations on objects, including lists, numbers, characters, strings, vectors, symbols, and boxes. The first section describes generic equivalence predicates for comparing two objects, and predicates for determining the *type* of an object. Later sections describe procedures that deal primarily with one of the object types mentioned above. There is no section treating operations on procedures, since the only operation defined specifically for procedures is application, and this is described in Chapter 4. Operations on ports are covered in the more general discussion of input and output in Chapter 6.

5-1 Generic Equivalence and Type Predicates

This section describes the basic Scheme predicates (procedures returning one of the boolean values #t or #f) for determining the type of an object or the equivalence of two objects. The equivalence predicates eq?, eqv?, and equal? are discussed first, followed by the type predicates.

(eq? obj_1 obj_2)   procedure

> returns: #t if obj_1 and obj_2 are identical, #f otherwise

> In most Scheme systems, two objects are considered identical if they are represented internally by the same pointer value, and distinct (not identical) if they are represented internally by different pointer values, although other criteria, such as time-stamping, are possible.

> Although the particular rules for object identity vary from system to system, the following rules always hold:

> - Two objects of different types are distinct, except that characters may not be implemented in some Scheme systems as a type distinct from all other types; for example, characters may be represented by a range of integers or by strings of length one.

> - Also, two objects with different contents or values are distinct.

- The boolean object #t is identical to itself wherever it appears. For example, the value returned by (= 3 3) is identical to the value returned by (string? "hi"). Similarly, the boolean value #f is identical to itself, and the empty list () is identical to itself. Furthermore, #t is distinct from #f and from (). Scheme does not specify whether #f and () are identical or distinct.

- Two interned symbols (created by read or by symbol->string) are identical if and only if they print the same, *i.e.*, if and only if they have the same name (see symbol->name). Uninterned symbols with the same name may or may not be identical, but uninterned symbols with different names are distinct. Interned and uninterned symbols are distinct from each other.

- Two mutable objects created at different times by cons, vector, string, box, *etc.*, are distinct. One consequence is that cons or box, for example, may be used to create a new object distinct from all other objects.

Two numbers with the same value may or may not be identical, although every inexact number is distinct from every exact number.

Two procedures created by the same lambda expression at the same time are identical, but two procedures created by the same lambda expression at different times, or by similar lambda expressions, may or may not be identical.

```
(eq? 'a 3)         ⇒ #f
(eq? "hi" '(hi))   ⇒ #f
(eq? 9/2 7/2)      ⇒ #f
(eq? 3.4 53344)    ⇒ #f
(eq? '(a) '(b))    ⇒ #f

(eq? #t #t)        ⇒ #t
(eq? #t #f)        ⇒ #f

(eq? 'a 'a)        ⇒ #t
(eq? 'a 'b)        ⇒ #f


(eq? 'a (string->symbol "a"))             ⇒ #t
(eq? 'a (string->uninterned-symbol "a"))  ⇒ #f
(eq? (cons 'a 'b) (cons 'a 'b))           ⇒ #f
(let ([v (vector 1 2 3)])
  (eq? v v))                              ⇒ #t
```

```
(eq? 9/2 9/2)                              ⇒ unspecified
(eq? 3.4 (+ 3.0 .4))                       ⇒ unspecified
(eq? #\a #\a)                              ⇒ unspecified
(eq? car car)                              ⇒ #t
(eq? car cdr)                              ⇒ #f
(let ([f (lambda (x) x)])
   (eq? f f))                              ⇒ #t
(let ([f (lambda () (lambda (x) x))])
   (eq? (f) (f)))                          ⇒ unspecified
(eq? (lambda (x) x) (lambda (y) y))        ⇒ unspecified
```

(eqv? *obj*$_1$ *obj*$_2$)   procedure

returns: #t if *obj*$_1$ and *obj*$_2$ are operationally equivalent, #f otherwise

Operational equivalence is based on the external behavior of an object rather than its precise internal representation or pointer value. In general, two objects are operationally equivalent if they cannot be distinguished by any means other than by the use of eq?, eqv?, or by any means that ultimately employs one of these two predicates. Here are the rules for operational equivalence:

- Two identical objects (see eq? above) are operationally equivalent.

- Two objects of different types are operationally distinct (but see the discussion of characters under eq? above).

- Two numeric objects are operationally equivalent if they have the same value (according to =) and are both exact or inexact.

- Two character objects are operationally equivalent if they have the same value (according to char=?).

- Two mutable pairs, vectors, strings, or boxes are operationally equivalent only if mutation of one results in the mutation of the other, generally only if they are identical.

- An empty string is operationally equivalent to any other empty string, and an empty vector is operationally equivalent to any other empty vector. (Since all empty lists are identical, an empty list is operationally equivalent to any other empty list.)

- Two procedures are operationally equivalent if they accept the same arguments, return the same values, and perform the same side effects.

The predicate eqv? approximates operational equivalence, but it can fail to detect the operational equivalence of two procedures that are not identical. This is because determining the operational equivalence of procedures is generally impossible. eqv? can also fail to recognize the operational equivalence of two immutable pairs, strings, vectors, or boxes created at different times; this is because these objects may be stored in different locations, and determining their equivalence may be inordinately expensive. Immutable pairs, strings, vectors, or boxes may be introduced by some Scheme implementations for constants in Scheme code.

eqv? is generally more expensive than eq?, since it often requires the comparison of more than just the internal pointer value. For example, eqv? may be required to compare the digits of two large integers.

```
(eqv? 'a 3)        ⇒ #f
(eqv? "hi" '(hi))  ⇒ #f
(eqv? 9/2 7/2)     ⇒ #f
(eqv? 3.4 53344)   ⇒ #f
(eqv? '(a) '(b))   ⇒ #f

(eqv? #t #t)       ⇒ #t
(eqv? #t #f)       ⇒ #f

(eqv? 'a 'a)       ⇒ #t
(eqv? 'a 'b)       ⇒ #f


(eqv? 'a (string->symbol "a"))             ⇒ #t
(eqv? 'a (string->uninterned-symbol "a"))  ⇒ #f
(eqv? (cons 'a 'b) (cons 'a 'b))           ⇒ #f
(let ([v (vector 1 2 3)])
   (eqv? v v))                             ⇒ #t
(eqv? 9/2 9/2)                             ⇒ #t
(eqv? 3.4 (+ 3.0 .4))                      ⇒ #t
(eqv? #\a #\a)                             ⇒ #t

(eqv? car car)                             ⇒ #t
(eqv? car cdr)                             ⇒ #f
(let ([f (lambda (x) x)])
   (eqv? f f))                             ⇒ #t
(let ([f (lambda () (lambda (x) x))])
   (eqv? (f) (f)))                         ⇒ unspecified
```

```
(eqv? (lambda (x) x) (lambda (y) y))        ⇒ unspecified
```

(equal? obj_1 obj_2)   procedure

returns: #t if obj_1 and obj_2 have the same structure and contents, #f otherwise

In general, two objects are equal (have the same structure and contents) if they print the same. In particular, two objects are equal if they are operationally equivalent according to eqv?, strings and string=?, pairs whose cars and cdrs are equal, vectors of the same length whose corresponding elements are equal, or boxes whose boxed values are equal.

equal? is recursively defined and must compare not only numbers and characters for equivalence but also pairs, strings, vectors, and boxes. The result is that equal? is on the one hand more likely to return #t and on the other hand more likely to be slower than either eqv? or eq?.

```
(equal? "hi" '(hi))  ⇒ #f
(equal? '(a) '(b))   ⇒ #f
(equal? 'a 'a)       ⇒ #t
(equal? 'a 'b)       ⇒ #f

(equal? (cons 'a 'b) (cons 'a 'b))  ⇒ #t
(equal? "hi mom!" "hi mom!")        ⇒ #t
(equal? (vector 'a 'b 'c)
        (list->vector '(a b c)))    ⇒ #t

(equal? 9/2 9/2)        ⇒ #t
(equal? 3.4 (+ 3.0 .4))  ⇒ #t
(equal? #\a #\a)        ⇒ #t

(equal? car car)                            ⇒ #t
(equal? car cdr)                            ⇒ #f
(let ([f (lambda (x) x)])
   (equal? f f))                            ⇒ #t
(let ([f (lambda () (lambda (x) x))])
   (equal? (f) (f)))                         ⇒ unspecified
(equal? (lambda (x) x) (lambda (y) y))  ⇒ unspecified
```

(boolean? *obj*)   procedure

>   returns: #t if *obj* is either #t or #f, #f otherwise

>   Since () may be identical to #f, boolean? may return #t for () as well.

>>   (boolean? #t)   ⇒ #t
>>   (boolean? #f)   ⇒ #t
>>   (boolean? 't)   ⇒ #f
>>   (boolean? '())   ⇒ *unspecified*

(null? *obj*)   procedure

>   returns: #t if *obj* is the empty list, #f otherwise

>   null? is equivalent to (lambda (x) (eq? x '())).

>   Since () and #f may or may not be identical, null? may return #t for
>   #f.

>>   (null? '())   ⇒ #t
>>   (null? '(a))   ⇒ #f
>>   (null? (cdr '(a)))   ⇒ #t
>>   (null? 3)   ⇒ #f

(pair? *obj*)   procedure

>   returns: #t if *obj* is a pair, #f otherwise

>>   (pair? '(a b c))   ⇒ #t
>>   (pair? '(3 . 4))   ⇒ #t
>>   (pair? '())   ⇒ #f
>>   (pair? 3)   ⇒ #f

(list? *obj*)   procedure

>   returns: #t if *obj* is a pair or the empty list, #f otherwise

>   list? returns #t for both proper and improper lists.

>   list? is equivalent to (lambda (x) (or (pair? x) (null? x))).

>>   (list? '(a b c))   ⇒ #t
>>   (list? '(3 . 4))   ⇒ #t
>>   (list? '())   ⇒ #t
>>   (list? 3)   ⇒ #f

(atom? *obj*)   procedure

    returns: #t if *obj* is not a pair, #f otherwise

    atom? is equivalent to (lambda (x) (not (pair? x))). It is often more
convenient to write (atom? *x*) than to write (not (pair? *x*)).

        (atom? '(a b c)) ⇒ #f
        (atom? '(3 . 4)) ⇒ #f
        (atom? '())   ⇒ #t
        (atom? 3)   ⇒ #t

(number? *obj*)   procedure

    returns: #t if *obj* is numeric, #f otherwise

(complex? *obj*)   procedure

    returns: #t if *obj* is complex, #f otherwise

(real? *obj*)   procedure

    returns: #t if *obj* is real, #f otherwise

(rational? *obj*)   procedure

    returns: #t if *obj* is rational, #f otherwise

(integer? *obj*)   procedure

    returns: #t if *obj* is integer, #f otherwise

These predicates form a hierarchy: any integer is rational, any rational
is real, any real is complex, and any complex is numeric.

        (integer? 1901)   ⇒ #t
        (rational? 62)   ⇒ #t
        (complex? 124)   ⇒ #t

        (integer? 15/16)   ⇒ #f
        (rational? -2/3)   ⇒ #t
        (number? 17/2)   ⇒ #t

        (integer? -2.345)   ⇒ #f
        (real? 1678.2)   ⇒ #t
        (complex? .0005)   ⇒ #t

        (integer? 3+4i)   ⇒ #f
        (rational? -6+7i)   ⇒ #f
        (complex? 3.2-2.01i) ⇒ #t

(char? *obj*)   procedure

    returns: #t if *obj* is a character, #f otherwise

```
(char? #\a)  ⇒ #t
```

(string? _obj_)   procedure

    returns: #t if _obj_ is a string, #f otherwise

```
(string? "hi")  ⇒ #t
(string? 'hi)   ⇒ #f
```

(vector? _obj_)   procedure

    returns: #t if _obj_ is a vector, #f otherwise

```
(vector? '#())              ⇒ #t
(vector? (vector 'a 'b 'c)) ⇒ #t
(vector? '())              ⇒ #f
(vector? '(a b c))         ⇒ #f
(vector? "abc")            ⇒ #f
```

(symbol? _obj_)   procedure

    returns: #t if _obj_ is a symbol, #f otherwise

```
(symbol? 'a)    ⇒ #t
(symbol? "a")   ⇒ #f
(symbol? '(a))  ⇒ #f
```

(box? _obj_)   procedure

    returns: #t if _obj_ is a box, #f otherwise

```
(box? '#&a)     ⇒ #t
(box? 'a)       ⇒ #f
(box? (box 3))  ⇒ #t
```

(input-port? _obj_)   procedure

    returns: #t if _obj_ is an input port, #f otherwise

```
(input-port? (current-input-port))            ⇒ #t
(input-port? (open-output-file "myfile.ss"))  ⇒ #f
(input-port? (open-input-file "myfile.ss"))   ⇒ #t
```

(output-port? *obj*)   procedure

    returns: #t if *obj* is an output port, #f otherwise

       (output-port? (current-output-port))   ⇒ #t
       (output-port? (open-output-file "myfile.ss")) ⇒ #t
       (output-port? (open-input-file "myfile.ss"))   ⇒ #f

(procedure? *obj*)   procedure

    returns: #t if *obj* is a procedure, #f otherwise

Continuations and engines are themselves procedures, so procedure? can be used to distinguish them from nonprocedures but not from other procedures.

       (procedure? car)   ⇒ #t
       (procedure? 'car)   ⇒ #f
       (procedure? (lambda (x) x))   ⇒ #t
       (procedure? (call/cc (lambda (k) k))) ⇒ #t
       (procedure? (make-engine (lambda () 3))) ⇒ #t

5-2 Lists and Pairs

The pair, or *cons box*, is the most fundamental of Scheme's structured object types, as it is in Lisp. The most common use for pairs is to build lists, which are ordered sequences of pairs linked one to the next by the *cdr* field. The elements of the list occupy the *car* field of each pair. The cdr of the last pair in a *proper list* is the empty list, (); the cdr of the last pair in an *improper list* can be anything other than ().

    Pairs may be used to construct binary trees. Each pair in the tree structure is an internal node of the binary tree, while its car and cdr are the children of the node.

    Proper lists are printed as sequences of objects separated by white space (that is, blanks, tabs, and newlines) and enclosed in parentheses (brackets ([ ]) may also be used in some Scheme systems). For example, (1 2 3) and (a (nested list)) are proper lists. The empty list is written as ().

    Improper lists and trees require a slightly more complex syntax. A single pair is written as two objects separated by white space and a dot, *e.g.*, (a . b). This is referred to as *dotted-pair notation*. Improper lists and trees are also written in dotted-pair notation; the dot appears wherever necessary, *e.g.*, (1 2 3 . 4) or ((1 . 2) . 3). Of course, proper lists may be written in dotted-pair notation, with () to the right of the dot. For example, (1 2 3) may be written as (1 . (2 . (3 . ()))).

Unless otherwise stated, it is an error to pass an improper list to a procedure requiring a list argument. This error is not necessarily signaled but the behavior of the procedure on an improper list argument is unspecified (often, the last cdr is simply ignored, *i.e.*, treated as if it were ()).

It is possible to create a circular list or a cyclic graph by destructively altering the car or cdr field of a list, using set-car! or set-cdr!. Some of the procedures listed in this section may loop indefinitely when handed a cyclic structure.

(cons *obj*$_1$ *obj*$_2$)   procedure

>   returns: a new pair

>   cons is the pair constructor procedure. *obj*$_1$ becomes the car and *obj*$_2$ becomes the cdr of the new pair.

>   ```
>   (cons 'a '())     ⇒ (a)
>   (cons 'a '(b c))  ⇒ (a b c)
>   (cons 3 4)        ⇒ (3 . 4)
>   ```

(car *pair*)   procedure

>   returns: the car of *pair*

>   It is an error to ask for the car of the empty list.

>   ```
>   (car '(a))      ⇒ a
>   (car '(a b c))  ⇒ a
>   (car (cons 3 4)) ⇒ 3
>   ```

(cdr *pair*)   procedure

>   returns: the cdr of *pair*

>   It is an error to ask for the cdr of the empty list.

>   ```
>   (cdr '(a))      ⇒ ()
>   (cdr '(a b c))  ⇒ (b c)
>   (cdr (cons 3 4)) ⇒ 4
>   ```

(set-car! *pair obj*)   procedure

    returns: unspecified

    set-car! changes the car of *pair* to *obj*.

```
(let ([x '(a b c)])
  (set-car! x 1)
  x)                    ⇒ (1 b c)
```

(set-cdr! *pair obj*)   procedure

    returns: unspecified

    set-cdr! changes the cdr of *pair* to *obj*.

```
(let ([x '(a b c)])
  (set-cdr! x 1)
  x)                    ⇒ (a . 1)
```

(caar *pair*)   procedure
(cadr *pair*)   procedure
⋮
(cddddr *pair*)   procedure

    returns: the caar, cadr, ..., or cddddr of *pair*

This set of procedures are defined as the composition of up to four car's
and cdr's. The a's and d's between the c and d represent the application
of car or cdr in order from right to left. For example, the procedure cadr
applied to a pair yields the car of the cdr of the pair and is equivalent
to (lambda (x) (car (cdr x))).

```
(caar '((a)))       ⇒ a
(cadr '(a b c))     ⇒ b
(cdddr '(a b c d))  ⇒ (d)
(cadadr '(a (b c))) ⇒ c
```

(make-list *n*)   procedure
(make-list *n obj*)   procedure

    returns: a list of *n objs*

    n must be a nonnegative integer.

    If *obj* is omitted, the elements of the list are unspecified.

```
(make-list 0 '())   ⇒ ()
(make-list 3 0)     ⇒ (0 0 0)
(make-list 2 "hi")  ⇒ ("hi" "hi")
```

(list *obj* ...)   procedure

   returns: a list of *obj* ...

```
(list)        ⇒ ()
(list 1 2 3)  ⇒ (1 2 3)
(list 3 2 1)  ⇒ (3 2 1)
```

(list* *obj* ... *final-obj*)   procedure

   returns: a list of *obj* ... terminated by *final-obj*

If the objects *obj* ... are omitted, the result is simply *final-obj*. Otherwise, a list of *obj* ... is constructed, as with list, except that the final
cdr field is *final-obj* instead of (). If *final-obj* is not a list, the result is
an improper list.

```
(list* '())          ⇒ ()
(list* '(a b))       ⇒ (a b)
(list* 'a 'b 'c)     ⇒ (a b . c)
(list* 'a 'b '(c d)) ⇒ (a b c d)
```

(length *list*)   procedure

   returns: the number of elements in *list*

```
(length '())      ⇒ 0
(length '(a b c)) ⇒ 3
```

(list-ref *list* *n*)   procedure

   returns: the *n*th element (zero-based) of *list*

n must be a nonnegative integer strictly less than the length of *list*.

```
(list-ref '(a b c) 0)  ⇒ a
(list-ref '(a b c) 1)  ⇒ b
(list-ref '(a b c) 2)  ⇒ c
```

(list-tail *list n*)   procedure

> returns: the *n*th tail (zero-based) of *list*

n must be a nonnegative integer less than or equal to the length of *list*.

The result is not a copy; the tail is eq? to the *n*th cdr in cdr of *list*. *list*
may be an improper list, in which case the last tail is the terminating
object.

```
(list-tail '(a b c) 0)       ⇒ (a b c)
(list-tail '(a b c) 2)       ⇒ (c)
(list-tail '(a b c) 3)       ⇒ ()
(list-tail '(a b c . d) 2)   ⇒ (c . d)
(list-tail '(a b c . d) 3)   ⇒ d
```

(last-pair *list*)   procedure

> returns: the last pair of a *list*

list must not be empty.

last-pair returns the last pair (not the last element) of *list*. *list* may be
an improper list, in which case the last pair is the pair containing the
last element and the terminating object.

```
(last-pair '(a b c d))     ⇒ (d)
(last-pair '(a b c . d))   ⇒ (c . d)
```

(list-copy *list*)   procedure

> returns: a copy of *list*

list-copy returns a list equal? to *list*, using new pairs to reform the
top-level list structure.

```
(list-copy '(a b c))                          ⇒ (a b c)
(let ([ls '(a b c)])
   (equal? ls (list-copy ls)))                ⇒ #t
(let ([ls '(a b c)])
   (let ([ls-copy (list-copy ls)])
      (or (eq? ls-copy ls)
          (eq? (cdr ls-copy) (cdr ls))
          (eq? (cddr ls-copy) (cddr ls)))))   ⇒ #f
```

(tree-copy *tree*)   procedure

   returns: a copy of *tree*

   tree-copy returns a tree equal? to *tree*, using new pairs for all nonter-
   minal nodes.

```
(tree-copy '((a b) c . d))                    ⇒ '((a b) c . d)
(let ([tr '(a (b) c)])
   (equal? (tree-copy tr) tr))                 ⇒ #t
(let ([tr '(a (b) c)])
   (let ([tr-copy (tree-copy tr)])
      (or (eq? tr-copy tr)
          (eq? (cdr tr-copy) (cdr tr))
          (eq? (cadr tr-copy) (cadr tr))
          (eq? (cddr tr-copy) (cddr tr)))))    ⇒ #f
```

(append *list* ...)   procedure

(append! *list* ...)   procedure

   returns: the concatenation of the input lists

   append returns a new list consisting of the elements of the first list followed by the elements of the second list, the elements of the third list,
   and so on. The new list is made from new pairs for all arguments but
   the last; the last (which need not be a list) is merely placed at the end
   of the new structure.

   append! is similar to append but reuses the pairs in all of the arguments
   in forming the new list. That is, the last cdr of each list argument but
   the last is changed to point to the next list argument. If any argument
   but the last is the empty list, it is essentially ignored. The final argument
   (which need not be a list) is not altered.

```
(append '(a b c) '())      ⇒ (a b c)
(append '() '(a b c))      ⇒ (a b c)
(append '(a b) '(c d))     ⇒ (a b c d)
(append! '(a b) '(c d))    ⇒ (a b c d)
(let ([x '(a b)])
   (append x '(c d))
   x)                      ⇒ (a b)
(let ([x '(a b)])
   (append! x '(c d))
```

```
    x)                              ⇒ (a b c d)
```

(reverse *list*)   procedure

(reverse! *list*)   procedure

   returns: a list containing the elements of *list* in reverse order

   reverse returns a new list, while **reverse!** destructively reverses the
   argument list by reversing its links. **reverse!** is more efficient than
   reverse, since it avoids the allocation of new pairs, but its use can lead
   to confusing or incorrect results if used indiscriminately.

```
    (reverse '())                   ⇒ ()
    (reverse '(a b c))              ⇒ (c b a)
    (reverse! '())                  ⇒ ()
    (reverse! '(a b c))             ⇒ (c b a)
    (let ([x '(a b c)])
        (reverse x)
        x)                          ⇒ (a b c)
    (let ([x '(a b c)])
        (reverse! x)
        x)                          ⇒ (a)
    (let ([x '(a b c)])
        (set! x (reverse! x))
        x)                          ⇒ (c b a)
```

(memq *obj* *list*)   procedure

(memv *obj* *list*)   procedure

(member *obj* *list*)   procedure

   returns: the tail of *list* whose car is equivalent to *obj*, or #f

   These procedures traverse the argument *list* in order, comparing the
   elements of *list* against *obj*. If an object equivalent to *obj* is found, the
   tail of the list whose first element is that object is returned. If there
   is more than one object equivalent to *obj*, the first tail containing an
   equivalent object is returned. If no object equivalent to *obj* is found, #f
   is returned.

   The equivalence test for **memq** is **eq?**, for **memv** is **eqv?**, and for **member** is
   equal?.

These procedures are most often used as predicates, but their names do not end with a question mark because they return a useful true value in place of #t.

```
(memq 'a '(b c a d e))        ⇒ (a d e)
(memq 'a '(b c d e g))        ⇒ #f
(memq 'a '(b a c a d a))      ⇒ (a c a d a)
(memv 3.4 '(1.2 2.3 3.4 4.5)) ⇒ (3.4 4.5)
(memv 3.4 '(1.3 2.5 3.7 4.9)) ⇒ #f
(member '(b) '((a) (b) (c)))  ⇒ ((b) (c))
(member '(d) '((a) (b) (c)))  ⇒ #f
(member "b" '("a" "b" "c"))   ⇒ ("b" "c")
```

(remq *obj list*)	procedure
(remv *obj list*)	procedure
(remove *obj list*)	procedure
(remq! *obj list*)	procedure
(remv! *obj list*)	procedure
(remove! *obj list*)	procedure

returns: a list containing the elements of *list* with all occurrences of *obj* removed

These procedures traverse the argument *list*, removing any objects that are equivalent to *obj*. The elements remaining in the output list are in the same order as they appear in the input list.

The equivalence test for remq and remq!, is eq?, for remv and remv! is eqv?, and for remove and remove! is equal?.

remq!, remv! and remove! use pairs from the input list to build the output list. They are more efficient than their nondestructive counterparts, but confusing or incorrect results may occur if they are used indiscriminately.

```
(remq 'a '(a b a c a d))       ⇒ (b c d)
(remq 'a '(b c d))             ⇒ (b c d)
(remq! 'a '(a b a c a d))      ⇒ (b c d)
(remv 1/2 '(1.2 1/2 0.5 3/2 4)) ⇒ (1.2 0.5 3/2 4)
(remv! #\a '(#\a #\b #\c))     ⇒ (#\b #\c)
(remove '(b) '((a) (b) (c)))   ⇒ ((a) (c))
(remove! '(c) '((a) (b) (c)))  ⇒ ((a) (b))
```

(substq *new old tree*)	procedure
(substv *new old tree*)	procedure
(subst *new old tree*)	procedure
(substq! *new old tree*)	procedure
(substv! *new old tree*)	procedure
(subst! *new old tree*)	procedure

returns: a tree with *new* substituted for occurrences of *old* in *tree*

These procedures traverse *tree*, replacing all objects equivalent to the object *old* with the object *new*.

The equivalence test for substq and substq! is eq?, for substv and substv! is eqv?, and for subst and subst! is equal?.

substq!, substv!, and subst! perform the substitutions destructively.

```
(substq 'a 'b '((b c) b a))          ⇒ ((a c) a a)
(substv 2 1 '((1 . 2) (1 . 4) . 1))  ⇒ ((2 . 2) (2 . 4) . 2)
(subst 'a
       '(a . b)
       '((a . b) (c a . b) . c))      ⇒ (a (c . a) . c)
(let ([tr '((b c) b a)])
  (substq! 'a 'b tr)
  tr)                                 ⇒ ((a c) a a)
```

(assq *obj alist*)	procedure
(assv *obj alist*)	procedure
(assoc *obj alist*)	procedure

returns: first element of *alist* whose car is equivalent to *obj*, or #f

The argument *alist* must be an *association list*. An association list is a proper list whose elements are key-value pairs of the form (key . value). Associations are useful for storing information (values) associated with certain objects (keys).

These procedures traverse the association list, testing each key for equivalence with *obj*. If an equivalent key is found, the key-value pair is returned. Otherwise, #f is returned.

The equivalence test for assq is eq?, for assv is eqv?, and for assoc is equal?.

```
(assq 'b '((a . 1) (b . 2)))          ⇒ (b . 2)
(cdr (assq 'b '((a . 1) (b . 2))))    ⇒ 2
(assq 'c '((a . 1) (b . 2)))          ⇒ #f
(assv 2/3 '((1/3 . 1) (2/3 . 2)))     ⇒ (2/3 . 2)
(assv 2/3 '((1/3 . a) (3/4 . b)))     ⇒ #f
(assoc '(a) '(((a) . a) (-1 . b)))    ⇒ ((a) . a)
(assoc '(a) '(((b) . b) (a . c)))     ⇒ #f

(let ([alist '((2 . a) (3 . b))])
  (set-cdr! (assv 3 alist) 'c)
  alist)                              ⇒ ((2 . a) (3 . c))
```

(sort *predicate list*)   procedure
(sort! *predicate list*)   procedure

returns: a list containing the elements of **list** sorted according to *predicate*

predicate should be a procedure that expects two arguments and returns #t if its first argument must precede its second in the sorted list. Duplicate elements are not removed. **sort** and **sort!** perform stable sorts, *i.e.*, two elements are reordered only when necessary according to *predicate*.

sort! performs the sort destructively, using pairs from the input list to form the output list.

```
(sort < '(3 4 2 1 2 5))               ⇒ (1 2 2 3 4 5)
(sort > '(0.5 1/2))                   ⇒ (0.5 1/2)
(sort > '(1/2 0.5))                   ⇒ (1/2 0.5))
(list->string
   (sort char>?
         (string->list "hello")))     ⇒ "ollhe"
```

(merge *predicate list$_1$ list$_2$*)   procedure
(merge! *predicate list$_1$ list$_2$*)   procedure

returns: *list$_1$* merged with *list$_2$* in the order specified by *predicate*

predicate should be a procedure that expects two arguments and returns #t if its first argument must precede its second in the merged list. Duplicate elements are included in the merged list. **merge** and **merge!** are stable, in that items from *list$_1$* are placed in front of equivalent items from *list$_2$* in the output list.

`merge!` combines the lists destructively, using pairs from the input lists to form the output list.

```
(merge char<?
       '(#\a #\c)
       '(#\b #\c #\d))  ⇒  (#\a #\b #\c #\c #\d)
(merge <
       '(1/2 2/3 3/4)
       '(0.5 0.6 0.7))  ⇒  (1/2 0.5 0.6 2/3 0.7 3/4)
```

5-3 Numbers

Scheme provides operations on integers, ratios, real numbers, and imaginary numbers, although any particular implementation may support operations on a proper subset of these numeric types. Integer and rational arithmetic is typically supported to arbitrary precision; the size of an integer or of the denominator or numerator of a ratio is limited only by system storage constraints. Real arithmetic is typically supported by floating point operations provided by the host computer's hardware or by system software. Complex arithmetic is typically supported by system software representing imaginary numbers as ordered pairs (*real-part, imag-part*), where *real-part* and *imag-part* are floating point numbers, ratios, or integers.

The predicates `integer?`, `rational?`, `real?`, and `complex?` described in Section 5–1 are usually sufficient for distinguishing between the different numeric types. However, there is one other important property of a Scheme numeric object: its *exactness*. A numeric object is either *exact* or *inexact*, depending upon the quality of operations used to derive the number and the inputs to these operations. Where possible, the Scheme system attempts to combine exact numbers using exact operations. Rational numbers are usually, but not necessarily, exact; likewise, real numbers are usually, but not necessarily, inexact. The exactness of a complex numeric object depends upon the exactness of its real and imaginary parts. In practice, the internal representation for an exact quantity is as an integer or ratio, and the internal representation for an inexact quantity is as a floating point number, although other representations are possible.

Scheme numbers are written in a straightforward manner not too different from ordinary conventions for writing numbers. An integer is written as a sequence of numerals preceded by an optional sign and followed by an optional radix point and any number of zeros. For example, 3, +19., −100.000 and 208423089237489374 all represent integers.

A ratio is written as two sequences of numerals separated by a slash (/) and preceded by an optional sign. For example, 3/4, −6/5, and 1/1208203823 all represent ratios. A ratio is reduced immediately when it is read and may in fact reduce to an integer.

Real numbers are written in either fixed-point or scientific notation. In fixed-point notation, a real number is written as a sequence of numerals followed by a decimal point and another sequence of numerals, all preceded by an optional sign. In scientific notation, a real number is written as a sequence of numerals followed by an optional decimal point and a second string of numerals, followed by an exponent; an exponent is written as the letter e followed by a sequence of numerals preceded by an optional sign. For example, 1.5, 0.034, −10e10 and 1.5e−5 are valid floating-point numbers.

Complex numbers are written in either rectangular or polar form. In rectangular form, a complex number is written as ⟨number⟩⟨sign⟩⟨number⟩i, where ⟨number⟩ is any valid integer, rational, or real number, and ⟨sign⟩ is one of + or -. For example, 3+4i is a complex number written in rectangular form. In polar form, a complex number is written as ⟨number⟩@⟨number⟩. For example, 1.1@1.764 is a complex number written in polar form.

Numbers are written by default in base 10, although the special prefixes #b (binary), #o (octal), #d (decimal), and #x (hexadecimal) can be used to specify base 2, base 8, base 10, or base 16. For radix 16, the letters a through f or A through F serve as the additional numerals required to express digit values 10 through 15. For example, #b10101 is the binary equivalent of 21_{10}, #o72 is the octal equivalent of 58_{10}, and #xC7 is the hexadecimal equivalent of 199_{10}. In scientific notation the exponent is always written in base 10; furthermore, the exponent itself always specifies a power of 10.

Typically, integer or rational input is represented internally as exact, while real input is represented internally as inexact. It is possible to specify explicitly the exactness of a number with the prefixes #i (inexact) or #e (exact). This prefix may precede or follow the radix prefix, if any.

Some Scheme systems provide two sizes of floating point numbers to represent real quantities. The prefixes #s (short) and #l (long) may appear before or after any other prefixes to specify short or long floating point representation.

The remainder of this section describes procedures that operate on numbers. The type of numeric arguments accepted by these procedures is implied

When called with two or more arguments, - returns the result of subtracting the sum of the numbers num_2 ... from num_1.

```
(- 3)        ⇒ -3
(- -2/3)     ⇒ 2/3
(- 4 3)      ⇒ 1
(- 4 3 2 1)  ⇒ -2
```

(* *num* ...)   procedure

returns: the product of the arguments *num* ...

When called with no arguments, * returns 1.

```
(*)                  ⇒ 1
(* 1 2)              ⇒ 2
(* 3 4 5)            ⇒ 60
(apply * '(1 2 3 4 5))  ⇒ 120
```

(/ *num*$_1$ *num*$_2$ ...)   procedure

returns: see explanation

When called with one argument, / returns the reciprocal of num_1. That is, (/ num_1) is an idiom for (/ 1 num_1).

When called with two or more arguments, / returns the result of dividing num_1 by the product of the remaining arguments num_2 ....

```
(/ -17)       ⇒ -1/17
(/ 7/8)       ⇒ 8/7
(/ 8 2)       ⇒ 4
(/ 60 5 4 3 2)  ⇒ 1/2
```

(zero? *num*)   procedure

returns: #t if *num* is zero, #f otherwise

zero? is equivalent to (lambda (x) (= x 0)).

```
(zero? 0)          ⇒ #t
(zero? 1)          ⇒ #f
(zero? (- 3.0 3.0))  ⇒ #t
(zero? (+ 1/2 1/2))  ⇒ #f
(zero? 0+0i)       ⇒ #t
```

(positive? *real*)   procedure

    returns: #t if *real* is greater than zero, #f otherwise

    positive? is equivalent to (lambda (x) (> x 0)).

        (positive? 128) $\Rightarrow$ #t
        (positive? 0.0) $\Rightarrow$ #f
        (positive? 1.8e-15) $\Rightarrow$ #t
        (positive? -2/3) $\Rightarrow$ #f

(negative? *num*)   procedure

    returns: #t if *real* is less than zero, #f otherwise

    negative? is equivalent to (lambda (x) (< x 0)).

        (negative? -65) $\Rightarrow$ #t
        (negative? 0) $\Rightarrow$ #f
        (negative? -0.0121) $\Rightarrow$ #t
        (negative? 15/16) $\Rightarrow$ #f

(even? *int*)   procedure

    returns: #t if *int* is even, #f otherwise

        (even? 0) $\Rightarrow$ #t
        (even? 1) $\Rightarrow$ #f
        (even? 765432) $\Rightarrow$ #t
        (even? -120762398465) $\Rightarrow$ #f

(odd? *int*)   procedure

    returns: #t if *int* is odd, #f otherwise

        (odd? 0) $\Rightarrow$ #f
        (odd? 1) $\Rightarrow$ #t
        (odd? 765432) $\Rightarrow$ #f
        (odd? -120762398465) $\Rightarrow$ #t

(1+ *num*)   procedure
(1- *num*)   procedure

    returns: *num* plus 1 or *num* minus 1

    1+ is equivalent to (lambda (x) (+ x 1)); 1- is equivalent to (lambda (x) (- x 1)).

(expt-mod *int*$_1$ *int*$_2$ *int*$_3$)   procedure

> returns: *int*$_1$ raised to the *int*$_2$ power, modulo *int*$_3$

int$_1$, *int*$_2$ and *int*$_3$ must be nonnegative integers.

expt-mod performs its computation in such a way that the intermediate results are never much larger than *int*$_3$. This means that when *int*$_2$ is large, expt-mod is more efficient than the equivalent procedure (lambda (x y z) (modulo (expt x y) z)).

> (expt-mod 2 4 3) $\Rightarrow$ 1
> (expt-mod 2 76543 76543) $\Rightarrow$ 2

(random *int*)   procedure

> returns: a pseudorandom number between 0 (inclusive) and *int* (exclusive)

int must be a positive integer.

> (random 1) $\Rightarrow$ 0
> (random 1029384535235) $\Rightarrow$ 1029384535001, *every now and then*

(exact->inexact *num*)   procedure

> returns: an inexact representation for *num*

In a typical Scheme implementation, exact->inexact has the effect of converting from an integer or rational representation into a floating point representation.

(inexact->exact *num*)   procedure

> returns: an exact representation for *num*

In a typical Scheme implementation, inexact->exact has the effect of converting from a floating point representation into an integer or rational representation.

(rationalize *real*$_1$)   procedure

(rationalize *real*$_1$ *real*$_2$)   procedure

> returns: a rational representation of *real*$_1$

If *real*$_1$ is rational, rationalize returns *real*$_1$.

In the first form, if *real₁* is not rational, `rationalize` returns the rational number with the smallest denominator equal to *real₁*. The success of `rationalize` in this case depends upon real numbers being stored with finite precision; the result is such that the precision of the original representation is maintained.

In the second form, if *real₁* is not rational, `rationalize` returns the rational number with the smallest denominator that differs from *real₁* by no more than *real₂*.

```
(rationalize -15)          ⇒ -15
(rationalize 19/3)         ⇒ 19/3
(rationalize 0.5)          ⇒ 1/2
(rationalize 0.667 0.0001) ⇒ 667/1000
(rationalize 0.667 0.001)  ⇒ 2/3
```

(numerator *rat*)   procedure

    returns: the numerator of *rat*

If *rat* is an integer, the numerator is *rat*.

```
(numerator 9)     ⇒ 9
(numerator 2/3)   ⇒ 2
(numerator -9/4)  ⇒ -9
```

(denominator *rat*)   procedure

    returns: the denominator of *rat*

If *rat* is an integer, the denominator is 1.

```
(denominator 9)     ⇒ 1
(denominator 2/3)   ⇒ 3
(denominator -9/4)  ⇒ 4
```

(real-part *num*)   procedure

    returns: the real component of *num*

If *num* is real, the real component is *num*.

```
(real-part 3+4i)       ⇒ 3
(real-part -2.3+0.7i)  ⇒ -2.3
(real-part 17.2)       ⇒ 17.2
(real-part -17/100)    ⇒ -17/100
```

(imag-part *num*)   procedure

>   returns: the imaginary component of *num*
>
>   If *num* is real, the imaginary component is 0.
>
>    ```
>    (imag-part 3+4i)        ⇒ 4
>    (imag-part -2.3+0.7i)   ⇒ 0.7
>    (imag-part 17.2)        ⇒ 0
>    (imag-part -17/100)     ⇒ 0
>    ```

(make-rectangular *real*$_1$ *real*$_2$)   procedure

>   returns: a complex number with real component *real*$_1$ and imaginary component *real*$_2$
>
>    ```
>    (make-rectangular -2 7)       ⇒ -2+7i
>    (make-rectangular 2/3 -1/2)   ⇒ 2/3-1/2i
>    ```

(make-polar *real*$_1$ *real*$_2$)   procedure

>   returns: a complex number with magnitude *real*$_1$ and angle *real*$_2$
>
>    ```
>    (make-polar 7.2 -0.588)   ⇒ 7.2@-0.588
>    ```

(angle *num*)   procedure

>   returns: the angle part of the polar representation of *num*
>
>   The range of the result of is $-\pi$ (exclusive) to $+\pi$ (inclusive).
>
>    ```
>    (angle 7.3@1.5708)   ⇒ 1.5708
>    (angle 5.2)          ⇒ 0
>    ```

(magnitude *num*)   procedure

>   returns: the magnitude of the complex number *num*
>
>   magnitude is identical to abs, but is included for symmetry with angle.

(sqrt *num*)   procedure

>   returns: the principal square root of *num*
>
>   If *num* is a negative real number, the result is complex.
>
>    ```
>    (sqrt 4.84)    ⇒ 2.2
>    (sqrt -4.84)   ⇒ 0+2.2i
>    ```

(exp *num*)   procedure

(log *num*)   procedure

   returns: *e* to the *num* power (exp) or the natural log of *num* (log)

(sin *num*)   procedure

(cos *num*)   procedure

(tan *num*)   procedure

   returns: the sine, cosine, or tangent of *num*

   The argument is specified in radians.

(asin *num*)   procedure

(acos *num*)   procedure

   returns: the arc sine or the arc cosine of *num*

   The result is in radians.

(atan *num*)   procedure

(atan *real*$_1$ *real*$_2$)   procedure

   returns: see explanation

   When passed a single complex argument *num* (the first form), atan returns the arc tangent of *num*.

   When passed two real arguments (the second form), atan is equivalent to (lambda (x y) (angle (make-rectangular x y))).

5-4 Characters

Characters are atomic objects representing letters, digits, special symbols such as $ or -, and certain nongraphic control characters such as space and newline. Character are written with the #\ prefix. For graphic characters, the prefix is followed by the character itself. The written character representation of the letter A, for example, is #\A. Nongraphic characters may be written in this manner as well, but certain nongraphic characters have special names that allow them to be spelled out more clearly. For example, the written character representation for newline is #\newline. Listed below are the names for these nongraphic characters.

```
(char-numeric? #\7)      ⇒ #t
(char-numeric? #\2)      ⇒ #t
(char-numeric? #\X)      ⇒ #f
(char-numeric? #\space)  ⇒ #f
```

(char-lower-case? *letter*)   procedure

returns: #t if *letter* is lower-case, #f otherwise

If *letter* is not alphabetic, the result is unspecified.

```
(char-lower-case? #\r)  ⇒ #t
(char-lower-case? #\R)  ⇒ #f
(char-lower-case? #\8)  ⇒ unspecified
```

(char-upper-case? *letter*)   procedure

returns: #t if *letter* is upper-case, #f otherwise

If *letter* is not alphabetic, the result is unspecified.

```
(char-upper-case? #\r)  ⇒ #f
(char-upper-case? #\R)  ⇒ #t
(char-upper-case? #\8)  ⇒ unspecified
```

(char-whitespace? *char*)   procedure

returns: #t if *char* is whitespace, #f otherwise

Whitespace consists of spaces and newlines and possibly other non-graphic characters depending upon the Scheme implementation and the underlying operating system.

```
(char-whitespace? #\space)    ⇒ #t
(char-whitespace? #\newline)  ⇒ #t
(char-whitespace? #\Z)        ⇒ #f
```

(char-upcase *char*)   procedure

returns: the upper-case character equivalent to *char*

If *char* is a lower-case character, char-upcase returns the upper-case equivalent. If *char* is not a lower-case character, char-upcase returns char itself.

```
(char-upcase #\g)  ⇒ #\G
(char-upcase #\Y)  ⇒ #\Y
(char-upcase #\7)  ⇒ #\7
```

(char-downcase *char*)   procedure

> returns: the lower-case character equivalent to *char*

If *char* is an upper-case character, char-downcase returns the lower-case equivalent. If *char* is not an upper-case character, char-downcase returns char itself.

```
(char-downcase #\g)  ⇒ #\g
(char-downcase #\Y)  ⇒ #\y
(char-downcase #\7)  ⇒ #\7
```

(char->integer *char*)   procedure

> returns: an integer representation for *char*

char->integer is useful for performing table lookups, with the integer representation of *char* employed as an index into a table. The integer representation of a character is typically the integer code supported by the operating system for character input and output.

Although the particular representation employed depends on the Scheme implementation and the underlying operating system, the same rules regarding the relationship between character objects stated above under the description of char=? and its relatives is guaranteed to hold for the integer representations for characters as well.

The following examples assume that the integer representation is the ASCII code for the character.

```
(char->integer #\h)        ⇒ 104
(char->integer #\newline)  ⇒ 10
```

(integer->char *int*)   procedure

> returns: the character object corresponding to the integer *int*

This procedure is the functional opposite of char->integer. It is an error for *int* to be outside the range of valid integer character codes (0 to 255 for ASCII).

The following examples assume that the integer representation is the ASCII code for the character.

```
(integer->char 48)   ⇒ #\0
(integer->char 101)  ⇒ #\e
```

5-5 Strings

Strings are sequences of characters and are typically used as messages or character buffers. Scheme provides operations for creating strings, extracting characters from strings, obtaining substrings, concatenating strings, and altering the contents of a string.

A string is written as a sequence of characters surrounded by double quotes, *e.g.*, "hi there". A double quote may be introduced into a string by preceding it by a backward slash, *e.g.*, "two \"quotes\" within". A backwards slash may also be included by preceding it with a backward slash, *e.g.*, "a \\slash".

Strings are indexed by nonnegative integers; the index of the first element of any string is 0. The highest valid index for a given string is one less than its length.

(string=? *string₁ string₂ ...*)	procedure
(string<? *string₁ string₂ ...*)	procedure
(string>? *string₁ string₂ ...*)	procedure
(string<=? *string₁ string₂ ...*)	procedure
(string>=? *string₁ string₂ ...*)	procedure

returns: #t if the relation holds, #f otherwise

As with =, <, >, <=, and >=, these predicates express relationships among all of the arguments. For example, string>? tests if the lexicographic ordering of its arguments is monotonically decreasing.

The comparisons are based on the character predicates char=?, char<?, char>?, char<=?, and char>=?. Two strings are lexicographically equivalent if they are the same length and consist of the same sequence of characters according to char=?. If two strings differ only in length, the shorter string is considered to be lexicographically less than the longer string. Otherwise, the first character position at which the strings differ determines which string is lexicographically less than the other, according to char<?.

```
(string=? "mom" "mom")                    ⇒ #t
(string<? "mom" "mommy")                   ⇒ #t
(string>? "Dad" "Dad")                     ⇒ #f
(string=? "Mom and Dad" "mom and dad")    ⇒ #f
(string<? "a" "b" "c")                     ⇒ #t
```

(string-ci=? *string₁ string₂* ...)   procedure

(string-ci<? *string₁ string₂* ...)   procedure

(string-ci>? *string₁ string₂* ...)   procedure

(string-ci<=? *string₁ string₂* ...)   procedure

(string-ci>=? *string₁ string₂* ...)   procedure

returns: #t if the relation holds, #f otherwise

These predicates are case insensitive versions of string=?, string<?, string>?, string<=?, and string>=?. That is, the comparisons are based on the character predicates char-ci=?, char-ci<?, char-ci>?, char-ci<=?, and char-ci>=?.

```
(string-ci=? "Mom and Dad" "mom and dad")  ⇒ #t
(string-ci<=? "say what" "Say What!?")      ⇒ #t
(string-ci>? "N" "m" "L" "k")              ⇒ #t
```

(string *char* ...)   procedure

returns: string containing the characters *char* ...

```
(string)                ⇒ ""
(string #\a #\b #\c)    ⇒ "abc"
(string #\H #\E #\Y #\!) ⇒ "HEY!"
```

(make-string *int*)   procedure

(make-string *int char*)   procedure

returns: a string of length *int*

int must be a nonnegative integer.

If *char* is supplied, the string is filled with *char*, otherwise the characters contained in the string are unspecified.

```
(make-string 0)      ⇒ ""
(make-string 0 #\x)  ⇒ ""
(make-string 5 #\x)  ⇒ "xxxxx"
```

(string-length *string*)   procedure

returns: the number of characters in *string*

```
(string-length "abc")       ⇒ 3
(string-length "")          ⇒ 0
(string-length "hi there")  ⇒ 8
```

(string-ref *string* *n*)   procedure

returns: the *nth* character (zero-based) of *string*

n must be a nonnegative integer strictly less than the length of *string*.

```
(string-ref "hi there" 0)  ⇒ #\h
(string-ref "hi there" 5)  ⇒ #\e
```

(string-set! *string* *n* *char*)   procedure

returns: unspecified

n must be a nonnegative integer strictly less than the length of *string*.

```
(let ([str "hi there"])
  (string-set! str 6 #\r)
  (string-set! str 7 #\e)
  str)                      ⇒ "hi there"
```

(string-copy *string*)   procedure

returns: a new copy of *string*

```
(string-copy "abc")                 ⇒ "abc"
(let ([str "abc"])
  (eq? str (string-copy str)))      ⇒ #f
```

(string-append *string* ...)   procedure

returns: a new string formed by concatenating the strings *string* ...

```
(string-append)                          ⇒ ""
(string-append "abc" "def")              ⇒ "abcdef"
(string-append "Hey " "you " "there!")   ⇒ "Hey you there!"
```

(substring *string start end*)   procedure

returns: a copy of *string* from *start* (inclusive) to *end* (exclusive)

start and *end* must be nonnegative integers; *start* must be strictly less than the length of *string*, while *end* may be less than or equal to the length of *string*. If *end* ≤ *start*, a string of length zero is returned.

```
(substring "hi there" 0 1)        ⇒ "h"
(substring "hi there" 3 6)        ⇒ "the"
(substring "hi there" 5 5)        ⇒ ""
(let ([str "hi there"])
   (let ([end (string-length str)])
      (substring str 0 end)))      ⇒ "hi there"
```

(string-fill! *string char*)   procedure

returns: unspecified

string-fill! sets every character in *string* to *char*.

```
(let ([str (string-copy "sleepy")])
   (string-fill! str #\Z)
   str)                           ⇒ "ZZZZZZ"
```

(substring-fill! *string start end char*)   procedure

returns: unspecified

The characters of *string* from *start* (inclusive) to *end* (exclusive) are set to *char*.

start and *end* must be nonnegative integers; *start* must be strictly less than the length of *string*, while *end* may be less than or equal to the length of *string*. If *end* ≤ *start* , the string is left unchanged.

```
(let ([str (string-copy "a tpyo typo")])
   (substring-fill! str 2 6 #\X)
   str)                           ⇒ "a XXXX typo"
```

(string->list *string*)   procedure

> returns: a list of the characters in *string*

string->list allows a string to be converted into a list, so that Scheme's list-processing operations may be applied to the processing of strings.

```
(string->list "")                        ⇒ ()
(string->list "abc")                     ⇒ (#\a #\b #\c)
(apply char<? (string->list "abc"))      ⇒ #t
(map char-upcase (string->list "abc"))   ⇒ (#\A #\B #\C)
```

(list->string *list*)   procedure

> returns: a string of the characters in *list*

list must consist entirely of characters.

list->string is the functional opposite of string->list. A program might use both procedures together, first converting a string into a list, then operating on this list, and finally converting the list back into a string.

```
(list->string '())              ⇒ ""
(list->string '(#\a #\b #\c))   ⇒ "abc"
(list->string
  (map char-upcase
      (string->list "abc")))    ⇒ "ABC"
```

5-6 Vectors

Vectors are a more convenient or efficient data structure than lists for some applications. Whereas elements in a list are accessed sequentially, elements in a vector are accessed directly by their positions in the vector, their *indices*. The *length* of a vector in Scheme is the number of elements it contains. Elements have indices from 0 up to one less than the length of the vector.

As with lists, the elements of a vector may be of any type; a single vector may even hold more than one type of object.

Vectors are written as a sequence of objects separated by whitespace, preceded by the prefix #(and followed by). For example, a vector consisting of the elements a, b and c would be written as #(a b c).

The prefix may also specify the length of the vector; a prefix of the form #n(specifies that the length of the vector is n. If the length n is specified in the prefix, it is an error to supply more than n elements but not to supply less than n elements. If less than n elements are supplied, the last element supplied, if any, is repeated as many times as necessary. For example, #(a a a), #3(a a a), and #3(a) represent the same three-element vector. If no elements are supplied and n is not zero, the elements of the vector are unspecified.

Specifying the length explicitly can save keystrokes for vectors filled with identical elements, especially for large vectors, *e.g.*, #1000(a). It is also potentially more efficient to give the length explicitly, allowing the Scheme reader to construct a vector of the right size before reading the elements.

(vector *obj* ...)   procedure

>   returns: a vector of the objects *obj* ...

```
(vector)          ⇒ #()
(vector 'a 'b 'c)  ⇒ #(a b c)
```

(make-vector *n*)   procedure

(make-vector *n* *obj*)   procedure

>   returns: a vector of length *n*

n must be a nonnegative integer.

If *obj* is supplied, each element of the vector is filled with *obj*, otherwise the elements are unspecified.

```
(make-vector 0)      ⇒ #()
(make-vector 0 'a)   ⇒ #()
(make-vector 5 'a)   ⇒ #(a a a a a)
```

(vector-length *vector*)   procedure

>   returns: the number of elements in *vector*

```
(vector-length '#())              ⇒ 0
(vector-length '#(a b c))         ⇒ 3
(vector-length (vector 1 2 3 4))  ⇒ 4
(vector-length '#300())           ⇒ 300
```

`(vector-ref vector n)`   procedure

> returns: the nth element (zero-based) of *vector*

> n must be a nonnegative integer strictly less than the length of *vector*.

```
(vector-ref '#(a b c) 0)      ⇒ a
(vector-ref '#(a b c) 1)      ⇒ b
(vector-ref '#4(x y z w) 3)   ⇒ w
```

`(vector-set! vector n obj)`   procedure

> returns: unspecified

> n must be a nonnegative integer strictly less than the length of *vector*.

> vector-set! changes the nth element of *vector* to *obj*.

```
(let ([v (vector 'a 'b 'c 'd 'e)])
  (vector-set! v 2 'x)
  v)                              ⇒ #(a b x d e)
```

`(vector-copy vector)`   procedure

> returns: a copy of *vector*

> vector-copy creates a new vector of the same length and contents as *vector*. The elements themselves are not copied.

```
(vector-copy '#(a b c))       ⇒ #(a b c)
(let ([v '#(a b c)])
  (eq? v (vector-copy v)))    ⇒ #f
```

`(vector-fill! vector obj)`   procedure

> returns: unspecified

> vector-fill! replaces each element of *vector* with *obj*.

```
(let ([v (vector 1 2 3)])
  (vector-fill! v 0)
  v)                              ⇒ #(0 0 0)
```

`(vector->list vector)`   procedure

> returns: a list of the elements of *vector*

> vector->list provides a convenient method for applying list-processing operations to vectors.

```
(vector->list (vector))          ⇒ ()
(vector->list '#(a b c))         ⇒ (a b c)
(let ([v '#(1 2 3 4 5)])
   (apply * (vector->list v)))   ⇒ 120
```

(list->vector *list***)**   procedure

returns: a vector of the elements of *list*

list->vector is the functional opposite of vector->list. vector->list
and list->vector are often used in combination to take advantage of
a list-processing operation. A vector may be converted to a list with
vector->list, this list processed in some manner to produce a new list,
and the new list converted back into a vector with list->vector.

```
(list->vector '())                ⇒ #()
(list->vector '(a b c))           ⇒ #(a b c)
(let ([v '#(1 2 3 4 5)])
   (let ([ls (vector->list v)])
      (list->vector (map * ls ls))))) ⇒ #(1 4 9 16 25)
```

5-7 Symbols

Symbols are similar to strings, with one important difference; namely,
symbols that print the same are identical in the sense of eq? and so may
be compared for equivalence much more quickly than ordinary strings.
The reason is that the Scheme reader (see read) and the procedure
string->symbol catalog symbols in an internal symbol table, always returning the same symbol whenever the same name is encountered. The procedures string->uninterned-symbol and gensym avoid this process, creating a
new symbol each time; they are rarely useful except in generating unique
symbols in the definition of syntactic extensions to avoid identifier clashes.

The property that two symbols may be compared quickly for equivalence makes them ideally suited for use as identifiers in the representation of
Scheme programs, making the comparison of identifiers faster. This property also makes symbols useful for a variety of other purposes. For example,
symbols might be used as messages passed between procedures, or tags for
record structures (see record-case), or names for objects stored in an association list (see assq).

Symbols are written without double quotes or other bracketing characters. Parentheses, double quotes, spaces, and most other characters with a special meaning to the Scheme reader are not allowed within a symbol. It is safest to employ only the following set of characters.

- the lower case letters a through z,
- the upper case letters A through Z,
- the digits 0 through 9, and
- the characters ? ! . + - * / < = > $ % ^ & _ ~.

It is also safest to avoid using any character that may start a number as the first character of a symbol, although some Scheme systems interpret any sequence of the above characters that cannot be parsed as a number as a symbol. Notable exceptions to this rule of thumb are the symbols + and -, which are interpreted as symbols in all implementations of Scheme, and 1+ and 1-, which are interpreted as symbols in most implementations of Scheme.

Some implementations of Scheme allow characters outside of the set listed above to be included in a symbol, as double quotes are included in a string, by preceding the character with a backward slash, *e.g.*, a\ space, or by enclosing the entire symbol in vertical bars, *e.g.*, |hi, mom|.

Some implementations of Scheme associate *property lists* with symbols, allowing *key-value* pairs to be stored directly in the symbol. New key-value pairs may be placed in the property list or retrieved in a manner analogous to the use of association lists, using the procedures putprop and getprop. Property lists are often used to store information related to the symbol itself. For example, a natural language program might use symbols to represent words, using their property lists to store information about use and meaning.

(string->symbol *string*)   procedure

   returns: a symbol whose name is *string*

   symbol->string records all symbols it creates in an internal table that it shares with the system reader, read. If a symbol whose name is equivalent to string (according to the predicate string=?) already exists in the table, this symbol is returned. Otherwise, a new symbol is created with *string* as its name; this symbol is entered into the table and returned.

   The system reader arranges to convert all symbols to a single case (lower case is assumed in this book), before entering them into the internal table. string->symbol does not. Thus, it is possible to produce symbols in either lower or upper case, or even mixed-case symbols, using string->symbol.

```
(string->symbol "x")        ⇒ x
(string->symbol "X")        ⇒ X
(eq? (string->symbol "x") 'x) ⇒ #t
(eq? (string->symbol "X") 'x) ⇒ #f
(eq? (string->symbol "x")
     (string->symbol "x"))  ⇒ #t
```

(string->uninterned-symbol *string***)**   procedure

returns: a new, unique symbol whose name is *string*

Each call to string->uninterned-symbol returns a new symbol. The name *uninterned symbol* comes from the fact that these symbols are not recorded in the internal symbol table. Uninterned symbols are primarily useful for generating lexical identifiers for use in program transformation systems or program improvers.

As with string->symbol, no case conversion is performed.

See also the procedure gensym.

```
(string->uninterned-symbol "g")        ⇒ g
(string->uninterned-symbol "G")        ⇒ G
(eq? (string->uninterned-symbol "g") 'g) ⇒ #f
(eq? (string->uninterned-symbol "g")
     (string->uninterned-symbol "g"))  ⇒ #f
```

(gensym)   procedure

returns: a new uninterned symbol

gensym maintains an internal counter and creates a new uninterned symbol with a different name each time it is applied. gensym returns a symbol with a different name, not because this makes the symbol unique (which is insured just by creating an uninterned symbol) but because this behavior is more suited to the generation of code or other uses for uninterned symbols where the symbols are likely to be printed. It is much easier to debug a program that creates uninterned symbols if each distinct uninterned symbol looks distinct as well.

The following examples assume that gensym creates symbols with a prefix of "G" and an integer suffix starting at zero.

```
(gensym)                        ⇒ G0
(gensym)                        ⇒ G1
(eq? (gensym) (gensym))  ⇒ #f
```

(uninterned-symbol? *symbol***)**   procedure

returns: #t if *symbol* is an uninterned symbol, #f otherwise

```
(uninterned-symbol? (string->symbol "z"))             ⇒ #f
(uninterned-symbol? (string->uninterned-symbol "z"))  ⇒ #t
(uninterned-symbol? 'a)                               ⇒ #f
```

(symbol->string *symbol***)**   procedure

returns: a string, the name of *symbol*

The string returned by symbol->string for a symbol created by an earlier call to string->symbol or string->uninterned-symbol may or may not be the same string (by eq?) as the string passed to string->symbol or string->uninterned-symbol. That is, an implementation is free to copy or not to copy a string it uses as the name of a symbol. As a result, unpredictable things can happen if a string passed to either string->symbol or string->uninterned-symbol is altered with string-set! or by any other means.

```
(symbol->string 'xyz)                ⇒ "xyz"
(symbol->string (string->symbol "Hi")) ⇒ "Hi"
```

(putprop *symbol key value***)**   procedure

returns: unspecified

putprop associates *value* with *key* on the property list of *symbol*. *key* and *value* may be any type of object, although *key* is typically a symbol.

putprop may be used to establish a new property or to change an existing property. It may also be used to remove a property by supplying #f for *value*.

See the examples under getprop below.

(getprop *symbol key*)   procedure

returns: the value associated with *key* on the property list of *symbol*

getprop searches the property list of *symbol* for a key identical to *key* (in the sense of eq?), and returns the value associated with this key, if any. If there is no value associated with *key* on the property list of *symbol*, getprop returns #f.

```
(putprop 'fred 'species 'snurd)
(putprop 'fred 'age 4)
(putprop 'fred 'colors '(black white))

(getprop 'fred 'species)           ⇒ snurd
(getprop 'fred 'colors)            ⇒ (black white)
(getprop 'fred 'nonkey)            ⇒ #f

(putprop 'fred 'species #f)
(getprop 'fred 'species)           ⇒ #f
```

5-8 Boxes

Boxes are single-cell objects that are primarily useful for providing an "extra level of indirection." This extra level of indirection is typically used to allow more than one body of code or data structure to share a reference, or pointer, to an object. For example, boxes may be used to implement *call-by-reference* semantics in an interpreter for a language employing this parameter passing discipline.

Boxes are written with the prefix #& (pronounced "hash-ampersand"). For example, #&(a b c) is a box holding the list (a b c).

(box *obj*)   procedure

returns: a new box containing *obj*

```
(box 'a)                ⇒ #&a
(box (box '(a b c)))    ⇒ #&#&(a b c)
```

(unbox *box*)   procedure

returns: contents of *box*

```
(unbox #&a)              ⇒ a
(unbox #&#&(a b c))      ⇒ #&(a b c)
(let ([b (box "hi")])
  (unbox b))             ⇒ "hi"
```

(set-box! *box obj*)   procedure

returns: unspecified

set-box! sets the contents of *box* to *obj*.

```
(let ([b (box 'x)])
  (set-box! b 'y)
  b)                 ⇒ #&y

(let ([incr!
       (lambda (x)
         (set-box! x (+ (unbox x) 1)))])
  (let ([b (box 3)])
    (incr! b)
    (unbox b)))                            ⇒ 4
```

Chapter 6: Input and Output Operations

This chapter describes input and output operations. All input and output operations are performed through *ports*. A port is a pointer into a (possibly infinite) stream of characters (typically a file), an opening through which programs may draw characters or objects from the stream or place characters or objects into the stream. Ports correspond to streams in Common Lisp or file pointers in Pascal [8].

Ports are first-class objects, just like any other object in Scheme. Like procedures, ports do not have a printed representation the way strings and numbers do, so they are shown here with the notation #<port>. There are initially two ports in the system, the current input port and the current output port. These ports usually point to the terminal input and output streams. Several ways to create new ports are provided.

Input ports often point to a finite stream, *e.g.*, an input file stored on disk. If one of the input operations `read` or `read-char` is asked to read from a port that has reached the end of a finite stream, it returns a special *eof object*. (The term *eof* stands for *end-of-file*, and is used even though the port may point to something other than a file). The predicate `eof-object?` may be used to determine if an object returned from `read` or `read-char` is an eof object.

Chez Scheme provides string ports as well as file ports; other types of ports are possible as well.

6-1 Input Operations

This section describes operations for manipulating input ports.

(`current-input-port`)   procedure

    returns: the current input port

    Most operations dealing with input ports may be called with or without an explicit input port argument. If called without an explicit port argument, the current input port is used. For example, (`read-char`) and (`read-char` (`current-input-port`)) both return the next character from the current input port. By default, the current input port points to the keyboard input stream.

(open-input-file *filename*)   procedure

   returns: a new input port

   filename must be a string.

   open-input-file creates a new input port for the file named by *filename*. An error is signaled if the file does not exist or cannot be opened for input.

   See the example given for close-input-port.

(close-input-port *input-port*)   procedure

   returns: unspecified

   close-input-port closes an input port. Once an input port has been closed, no more input operations may be performed on that port. Because the operating system may place limits on the number of ports open at one time or restrict access to an open port, it is a good practice to close any port that will no longer be used for input or output.

   It is not an error to close a port that has already been closed; doing so has no effect.

   The following shows the use of open-input-file and close-input-port to gather a list of objects from the file "myfile.ss". It is functionally equivalent to the example given for call-with-input-file below.

```
(let ([p (open-input-file "myfile.ss")])
  (let f ([x (read p)])
    (if (eof-object? x)
        (begin
          (close-input-port p)
          '())
        (cons x (f (read p)))))))
```

(call-with-input-file *filename* *proc*)   procedure

   returns: the result of invoking *proc*

   filename must be a string. *proc* must be a procedure of one argument.

`call-with-input-file` creates a new input port for the file named by *filename* and passes this port to *proc*. An error is signaled if the file does not exist or cannot be opened for input. If *proc* returns, `call-with-input-file` closes the input port and returns the value returned by *proc*.

`call-with-input-file` does *not* automatically close the input port if a continuation created outside of *proc* is invoked, since it is possible that another continuation created inside of *proc* will be invoked at a later time, returning control to *proc*. If *proc* does not return, an implementation is free to close the input port only if it can prove the input port is no longer accessible.

`call-with-input-file` might be defined as follows.

```
(define call-with-input-file
  (lambda (filename proc)
    (let ([p (open-input-file filename)])
      (let ([v (proc p)])
        (close-input-port p)
        v))))
```

The following example shows the use of `call-with-input-file` to gather a list of objects from the file `"myfile.ss"`. It is functionally equivalent to the example given for `close-input-port` above.

```
(call-with-input-file "myfile.ss"
  (lambda (p)
    (let f ([x (read p)])
      (if (eof-object? x)
          '()
          (cons x (f (read p)))))))
```

(open-input-string *string*)   procedure

  returns: a new string input port

A string input port is similar to a file input port, except that characters and objects drawn from the port come from *string* rather than from a file.

A string port is at "end of file" when the port reaches the end of the string. It is not necessary to close a string port.

```
(let ([p (open-input-string "hi mom!")])
  (let ([x (read p)])
    (list x (read p))))                    ⇒ (hi mom!)
```

(read)   procedure

(read *input-port*)   procedure

   returns: the next object from *input-port*

   If *input-port* is not supplied, it defaults to the current input port.

   If *input-port* is at end-of-file, an eof object is returned.

   See the examples given for close-input-port and call-with-input-file.

(read-char)   procedure

(read-char *input-port*)   procedure

   returns: the next character from *input-port*

   If *input-port* is not supplied, it defaults to the current input port.

   If *input-port* is at end-of-file, an eof object is returned.

   See the examples given for unread-char and write-char.

(unread-char *char*)   procedure

(unread-char *char input-port*)   procedure

   returns: unspecified

   If *input-port* is not supplied, it defaults to the current input port.

   It is an error to call unread-char twice on the same port without an
   intervening call to read-char.

   char may or may not be ignored, depending upon the implementation.
   In any case, it is an error for *char* not to be last character read from the
   port.

   unread-char is provided for applications requiring one character of lookahead. One character of lookahead is required, for example, in the procedure read-word defined below. read-word returns the next word from
   an input port as a string, where a word is defined to be a sequence of
   alphabetic characters. Since it does not know until it reads one character too many that it has read the entire word, it must use unread-char
   to return the character to the input port.
```
```

```
(define read-word
  (lambda (p)
    (list->string
      (let f ([c (read-char p)])
        (cond
          [(eof-object? c) '()]
          [(char-alphabetic? c)
           (cons c (f (read-char p)))]
          [else
           (unread-char c p)
           '()]))))))
```

By virtue of its definition, read-word returns an empty string if the next character on the port is not alphabetic, without having used up any characters from the port.

(eof-object? *obj*)   procedure

returns: #t if *obj* is an eof object, #f otherwise

This predicate is used to determine when an input port has reached the end of input.

(char-ready?)   procedure

(char-ready? *input-port*)   procedure

returns: #t if a character is available on *input-port*, #f otherwise

If *input-port* is not supplied, it defaults to the current input port.

If char-ready? returns #t, then the next read-char operation on *input-port* will not be delayed.

If *input-port* is at end-of-file, char-ready? returns #t.

char-ready? allows a program to look for character input on an interactive port without hanging.

(clear-input-port)   procedure

(clear-input-port *input-port*)   procedure

returns: unspecified

If *input-port* is not supplied, it defaults to the current input port.

Ports are typically buffered internally for efficiency. `clear-input-port` discards any characters in the buffer associated with *input-port*. This may be necessary, for example, to clear any type-ahead from the keyboard in preparation for an urgent query.

6-2 Output Operations

This section describes operations for manipulating output ports.

(current-output-port)   procedure

    returns: the current output port

Most operations dealing with output ports may be called with or without an explicit output port argument. If called without an explicit port argument, the current output port is used. Thus, (display *obj*) and (display *obj* (current-output-port)) both display *obj* on the current output port. By default, the current output port points to the keyboard output stream.

(open-output-file *filename*)   procedure

    returns: a new output port

filename must be a string.

open-output-file creates a new output port for the file named by *filename*. An error is signaled if the file cannot be opened for output.

See the example given for `close-output-port`.

(close-output-port *output-port*)   procedure

    returns: unspecified

close-output-port closes an output port. Once an output port has been closed, no more output operations may be performed on that port. Because the operating system may place limits on the number of ports open at one time or restrict access to an open port, it is a good practice to close any port that will no longer be used for input or output. Also, because the system may buffer output for efficiency, some of the output may not appear on the file until the file has been closed (see flush-output-port).

It is not an error to close a port that has already been closed; doing so has no effect.

The following shows the use of `open-output-file` and `close-output-port` to write a list of objects (the value of `list-to-be-printed`), separated by newlines, to the file `"myfile.ss"`. It is functionally equivalent to the example given for `call-with-output-file` below.

```
(let ([p (open-output-file "myfile.ss")])
  (let f ([ls list-to-be-printed])
    (unless (null? ls)
      (write (car ls) p)
      (newline p)
      (f (cdr ls))))
  (close-output-port p))
```

(`call-with-output-file` *filename proc*)   procedure

returns: the result of invoking *proc*

filename must be a string. *proc* must be a procedure of one argument.

`call-with-output-file` creates a new output port for the file named by *filename* and passes this port to *proc*. An error is signaled if the file cannot be opened for output. If *proc* returns, `call-with-output-file` closes the output port and returns the value returned by *proc*.

`call-with-output-file` does *not* automatically close the output port if a continuation created outside of *proc* is invoked, since it is possible that another continuation created inside of *proc* will be invoked at a later time, returning control to *proc*. If *proc* does not return, an implementation is free to close the output port only if it can prove the output port is no longer accessible.

`call-with-output-file` might be defined as follows.

```
(define call-with-output-file
  (lambda (filename proc)
    (let ([p (open-output-file filename)])
      (let ([v (proc p)])
        (close-output-port p)
        v))))
```

The following shows the use of `call-with-output-file` to write a list of objects (the value of `list-to-be-printed`), separated by newlines, to the file `"myfile.ss"`. It is functionally equivalent to the example given for `close-output-port` above.

```
(call-with-output-file "myfile.ss"
  (lambda (p)
    (let f ([ls list-to-be-printed])
      (unless (null? ls)
        (write (car ls) p)
        (newline p)
        (f (cdr ls))))))
```

`(open-output-string)`   procedure

returns: a new string output port

A string output port is similar to a file output port, except that characters and objects written to the port are placed in a string (which grows as needed) rather than to a file.

It is not necessary to close a string port.

The string built by writing to a string output port may be obtained with `get-output-string`. See the example given for `get-output-string` below.

`(get-output-string` *string-output-port*`)`   procedure

returns: the string associated with *string-output-port*

As a side effect, `get-output-string` resets *string-output-port* so that subsequent objects written to *string-output-port* are placed into a fresh string.

```
(let ([p (open-output-string)])
  (write 'hi p)
  (write-char #\space p)
  (write 'mom! p)
  (get-output-string p))        ⇒ "hi mom!"
```

(write *obj*)   procedure

(write *obj output-port*)   procedure

> returns: unspecified

If *output-port* is not supplied, it defaults to the current output port.

write prints *obj* on *output-port* in such a way that it can later be read by the procedure read, unless it contains unprintable objects such as procedures, ports, or symbols containing nonstandard characters. Strings are printed within quote marks, using slashes where necessary, and characters are printed with the "#\" notation (assuming characters are implemented as a type distinct from other types).

write is intended primarily for output that must show the distinction between symbols and strings and between sequences of characters and other objects or for output intended to be read subsequently with read.

write corresponds to prin1 in most Lisp systems.

(display *obj*)   procedure

(display *obj output-port*)   procedure

> returns: unspecified

If *output-port* is not supplied, it defaults to the current output port.

display prints *obj* on *output-port* in a more human-readable fashion. Strings are printed without quote marks or slashes, and characters are printed without the "#\" notation (assuming characters are implemented as a type distinct from other types).

display is intended primarily for printing messages or other output that need not show precisely the type of object being printed.

display corresponds to princ in most Lisp systems.

(pretty-print *obj*)   procedure

(pretty-print *obj output-port*)   procedure

> returns: unspecified

If *output-port* is not supplied, it defaults to the current output port.

pretty-print is similar to write except that it uses any number of spaces and newlines in order to print *obj* in a style that is pleasing to look at and which shows the nesting level via indentation. Since it is intended primarily for formating Scheme programs that may be subsequently loaded or compiled, pretty-print follows write in the treatment of strings and characters.

(write-char *char*)   procedure

(write-char *char output-port*)   procedure

   returns: unspecified

If *output-port* is not supplied, it defaults to the current output port.

write-char writes the single character *char* on *output-port* as itself, *i.e.*, without the "#\" notation.

The following example copies the contents of one file to another file, one character at a time.

```
(call-with-input-file
  (lambda (ip)
    (call-with-output-file
      (lambda (op)
        (do ([c (read-char ip) (read-char ip)])
            ((eof-object? c))
          (write-char c op))))))
```

(newline)   procedure

(newline *output-port*)   procedure

   returns: unspecified

If *output-port* is not supplied, it defaults to the current output port.

newline sends a newline character to *output-port*.

newline may be defined as follows.

```
(lambda args (apply write-char #\newline args))
```

`(clear-output-port)`   procedure

`(clear-output-port` *output-port*`)`   procedure

>   returns: unspecified

If *output-port* is not supplied, it defaults to the current output port.

Ports are typically buffered internally for efficiency. `clear-output-port` discards any characters in the buffer associated with *output-port*. This may be necessary, for example, to clear any pending output on an interactive port in preparation for an urgent message.

`(flush-output-port)`   procedure

`(flush-output-port` *output-port*`)`   procedure

>   returns: unspecified

If *output-port* is not supplied, it defaults to the current output port.

Ports are typically buffered internally for efficiency. `flush-output-port` forces any characters in the buffer associated with *output-port* to be printed immediately.

The current output port is automatically flushed after a newline and before input from the current input port; all ports are automatically flushed when they are closed. `flush-output-port` may be necessary, however, to force a message without a newline to be sent to the current input port, or to force output to appear on a file before it is closed.

6-3 Formatted Output

`(format` *format-string obj* `...)`   procedure

>   returns: formatted output string

`format` constructs an output string from *format-string* and the objects *obj* .... Characters are copied from *format-string* to the output string from left to right, until *format-string* is exhausted. During this operation, if `format` encounters a two-character sequence of the form "˜⟨char⟩" (tilde followed by the character ⟨char⟩), this sequence is replaced in the output string as follows:

~s is replaced by the printed representation of the next *obj*, which may be any object, in machine-readable format, as with write. "s" is used for compatibility with Common Lisp, where it stands for "s-expression," the Lisp term for object.

~a is replaced by the printed representation of the next *obj*, which may be any object, in human-readable format, as with display. "a" is used for compatibility with Common Lisp, where it stands for "ascii."

~c is replaced by the next *obj*, which must be a character, as with write-char.

~% is replaced by a newline character, as with newline.

~~ is replaced by a single tilde.

format is similar to but less powerful than Common Lisp's format.

An error is signaled if more or fewer *objs* are given than required by *format-string*, or if *format-string* ends in a tilde.

```
(format "hi there")                 ⇒ "hi there"
(format "hi ~s" 'mom)               ⇒ "hi mom"
(format "hi ~s" "mom")              ⇒ "hi \"mom\""
(format "hi ~s~s" 'mom #\!)         ⇒ "hi mom#\\!"
(format "hi ~a" "mom")              ⇒ "hi mom"
(format "hi ~s~a" 'mom #\!)         ⇒ "hi mom!"
(format "hi ~s~c" 'mom #\!)         ⇒ "hi mom!"
(format "~s.~s" 3 4)                ⇒ "3.4"
(format "~s" 12345)                 ⇒ "12345"
(format "line one,~%line two.")     ⇒ "line one,
                                       line two."
```

format could be defined roughly as follows (error checking has been omitted to simplify the code).

```
(define format
  (lambda (format-string . objects)
    (let ([ip (open-input-string format-string)])
      (let ([op (open-output-string)])
        (let f ([c (read-char ip)] [ls objects])
          (cond
            [(eof-object? c)
```

```
              (get-output-string op)]
            [(char=? c #\~)
             (case (read-char ip)
               [#\s
                (write (car ls) op)
                (f (read-char ip) (cdr ls))]
               [#\a
                (display (car ls) op)
                (f (read-char ip) (cdr ls))]
               [#\c
                (write-char (car ls) op)
                (f (read-char ip) (cdr ls))]
               [#\%
                (newline op)
                (f (read-char ip) ls)]
               [#\~
                (write-char #\~ op)
                (f (read-char ip) ls)])]
            [else
             (write-char c op)
             (f (read-char ip) ls)])))))))
```

(printf *format-string obj* ...)	procedure
(fprintf *output-port format-string obj* ...)	procedure

    returns: unspecified

Rather than returning a formatted string, these procedures write the formatted output to a port. printf always prints to the current output port.

Chapter 7: System Operations

This chapter describes various operations for interacting with Scheme, its compiler, and the operating system. These operations, more than any others in this book, are highly system dependent. Although most Scheme systems provide some or all of these operations in one form or another, their behavior may differ significantly in some circumstances from the descriptions herein.

7-1 Loading, Evaluation, and Compilation

(load *filename*)   procedure

(load *filename eval-proc*)   procedure

> returns: unspecified

> *filename* must be a string.

> This loads Scheme code from the file specified by *filename*. The file may contain either source or object code. If the file contains source code, load reads and evaluates the expressions in the file until it reaches end of file. If the file contains object code, the code must have been produced by the same version of Scheme you are currently using. If not, the result is unspecified.

> By default, load employs the eval procedure to evaluate the expressions in the file. If *eval-proc* is specified, load uses this procedure instead. This facilitates the implementation of new systems and the use of alternate evaluation mechanisms (such as the interpreter of Section 9–3) to be used for Scheme programs. The *eval-proc* can be put to other uses as well. For example, (load "myfile.ss" pretty-print) pretty-prints the file "myfile.ss" to the screen, and

```
(load "myfile.ss"
      (lambda (x)
         (write x)
         (newline)
         (eval x)))
```

prints each expression before evaluating it.

(eval *exp***)**   procedure

   returns: the result of evaluating *obj*

eval is intended to support the writing of interactive tools such as read-evaluate-print loops. It is not intended for use in applications that build an expression "on the fly" and evaluate it; programs that do so can often be rewritten to use first-class procedures, resulting in clearer and more efficient code.

eval in Scheme typically compiles *exp* and executes the resulting object code, rather than interpreting the expression directly as is done in most Lisp systems.

```
(eval 3)              ⇒ 3
(eval '(+ 3 4))       ⇒ 7
(eval ''(+ 3 4))      ⇒ (+ 3 4)
(eval (list '+ 3 4))  ⇒ 7
```

(expand *exp***)**   procedure

   returns: expanded expression

expand calls the system syntax expander to expand any syntactic extensions within *exp*.

```
(expand 3)                 ⇒ 3
(expand 'a)                ⇒ a
(expand '(let ([x 3]) x))  ⇒ ((lambda (x) x) 3)
(expand                        ((lambda (x)
  '(let* ([x a] [y b])    ⇒       ((lambda (y) (if x y #f)) b))
    (and x y)))                  a)
```

(expand-once *exp***)**   procedure

   returns: expanded expression

expand calls the system syntax expander to expand *exp* one level. If *exp* is not a syntactic extension, it is returned unchanged.

```
(expand-once 3)                ⇒ 3
(expand-once 'a)               ⇒ a
(expand-once '(let ([x 3]) x))  ⇒ ((lambda (x) x) 3)

(expand-once                       (let ([x a])
  '(let* ([x a] [y b])     ⇒         (let* ([y b])
     (and x y)))                       (and x y)))
```

(compile-file *filename*)   procedure

   returns: unspecified

The normal evaluation process proceeds in two steps: compilation and execution. compile-file performs the compilation process for an entire source file, producing an object file. When the object file is subsequently loaded (see load), the compilation process is not necessary, and the file typically loads several times faster.

In *Chez* Scheme, an extension of ".ss" is assumed for the input (source) filename; this extension is replaced by an extension of ".so" in the output (object) filename. The input filename may be entered with or without the ".ss" extension. For example, (compile-file "myfile") produces an object file with the name "myfile.so" from the source file named "myfile.ss".

(eval-when *situations exp* ...)   syntax

   returns: the value of the last *exp*

situations must be a list containing some combination of the symbols eval, compile, and load.

When source files are loaded (see load), the expressions in the file are read, compiled, and executed sequentially, so that each expression in the file is fully evaluated before the next one is read. When a source file is compiled (see compile-file), however, the expressions are read and compiled, *but not executed*, in sequence. This is a subtle distinction that matters only when the execution of one expression in the file affects the compilation of later expressions, *e.g.*, when the expression defines a new syntactic form (see extend-syntax).

For example, let's assume that we have a file containing the following two expressions:

```
(extend-syntax (reverse-define)
   [(reverse-define v x) (define x v)])
(reverse-define 3 three)
```

When loaded directly, this has the effect of defining a new syntactic
form, reverse-define, and binding at toplevel the identifier three to 3.
Unless the system or programmer takes steps to assure that the first
expression is fully executed before the second exression is compiled, the
syntax expander will not recognize reverse-define as a syntactic form
and will generate code for a procedure call to reverse-define instead of
generating code to define three to be 3. When the object file is subsequently loaded, the attempt to reference either identifier reverse-define
or three will (presumably) fail.

As it happens, when extend-syntax appears at toplevel as in the example
above, the compiler does indeed arrange to evaluate it before going on to
compile the remainder of the file, as well as generating the appropriate
code so that the syntactic form will be present as well when the object
file is subsequently loaded. This solves most, but not all, problems of
this nature, since most are related to the use of extend-syntax. However,
some problems are not so straightforwardly handled. For example, let's
assume that our file contains the following set of expressions:

```
(define simple?
   (lambda (x)
      (or (number? x)
          (and (pair? x)
               (memq (car x) '(+ - * /))
               (andmap simple? (cdr x)))))))
(extend-syntax (fold)
   [(fold exp)
    (with ([new-exp (if (simple? 'exp) (eval 'exp) 'exp)])
       new-exp)])
(define xyz (fold (* 3 (/ 2 (+ 7 2)))))
```

When loaded directly, this has the effect of defining simple? as a procedure, the syntactic-extension fold, and xyz as the ratio 2/3. Because the expression (* 3 (/ 2 (+ 7 2))) is simple according to
simple?, fold arranges to evaluate it during syntax expansion, so that
(define xyz (fold (* 3 (/ 2 (+ 7 2))))) expands to (define xyz 2/3).

(The advantage of using `fold` is to avoid repeated evaluation of a constant expression, say if the expression appeared within a loop.) If instead this file were compiled using `compile-file`, the compiler would arrange to define `fold` before continuing with the compilation, but it would not have defined `simple?`. Since `fold` requires `simple?` to be defined, the compilation of the next expression will fail. In this case it does not help to evaluate the syntactic extension alone, and the only solution is to specify with `eval-when` what expressions should or should not be evaluated during compilation.

The action of `eval-when` depends upon the *situations* argument and whether or not the expression *exp* is to be compiled to an object file or evaluated directly. Let's consider each of the possible situation specifiers `compile`, `load`, and `eval` individually.

> `compile`. The `compile` specifier is relevant only when the expression appears in a file currently being compiled. Its presence forces *exp* to be evaluated immediately.

> `load`. The `load` specifier is also relevant only when the expression appears in a file currently being compiled. Its presence forces *exp* to be compiled for execution when the object file being created is subsequently loaded.

> `eval`. The `eval` specifier is relevant only when the expression is being evaluated directly, *i.e.*, if it is typed at the keyboard or loaded from a source file. Its presence forces *exp* to be evaluated immediately.

Outside of any `eval-when` expression, the system treats all expressions as if they were wrapped in an `eval-when` with situations `load` and `eval`. This means that, by default, expressions typed at the keyboard or loaded from a source file are evaluated, and expressions appearing in a file to be compiled are not evaluated directly but are compiled for execution when the resulting object file is subsequently loaded. Top-level `extend-syntax` expressions are the only exception; these are treated as if wrapped in an `eval-when` with situations `compile`, `load`, and `eval`, forcing direct evaluation during compilation.

We could solve the second problem above by enclosing the definition of `simple?` in an `eval-when` as follows:

```
(eval-when (compile load eval)
   (define simple?
      (lambda (x)
         (or (number? x)
             (and (pair? x)
                  (memq (car x) '(+ - * /))
                  (andmap simple? (cdr x)))))))
```

thus forcing it to be evaluated before it is needed by `fold`.

Just as it is useful to add `compile` to the default `load` and `eval` situations, omitting options is also useful. Omitting one or more of `compile`, `load`, and `eval` has the effect of preventing the evaluation at the given time. Omitting all of the options has the effect of inhibiting evaluation altogether.

One common combination of situations is (`compile eval`), which by the inclusion of `compile` causes the expression to be evaluated directly by the compiler, and by the omission of `load` inhibits the generation of code by the compiler for execution when the file is subsequently loaded. This is typically used for the definition of syntactic extensions used only within the file in which they appear; in this case their presence in the object file is not necessary.

Another common situations list is (`compile`), which might be used to load a file of syntactic extensions kept separately for use during the compilation of a set of files. Omitting the `eval` option would be necessary in this case to prevent the file from being loaded more than once if this set of files were ever loaded directly.

Finally, one other common combination is (`load eval`), which might be useful for inhibiting the double evaluation (during the compilation of a file and again when the resulting object file is loaded) of syntactic extension definitions when the syntactic extensions are not needed within the file in which their definitions appear.

7-2 Top-Level Values

The operations described in this section allow the direct manipulation of top-level values for Scheme identifiers. They are intended to support the definition of interpreters or compilers for Scheme in Scheme as shown in Section 9–3. These procedures do not necessarily make sense in some Scheme systems that support multiple *top-level environments* to hold identifier bindings.

(define-top-level-value *symbol obj*)   procedure

> returns: unspecified

Definitions made with **define-top-level-value** are similar to top-level definitions made with **define**, except that *symbol* is evaluated by virtue of the fact that **define-top-level-value** is a procedure.

```
(begin
  (define-top-level-value 'xyz "hi")
  xyz)                              ⇒ "hi"
(let ([var 'xyz])
  (define-top-level-value var "mom")
  (list var xyz))                   ⇒ (xyz "mom")
```

(top-level-value *symbol*)   procedure

> returns: the top-level value of *symbol*

top-level-value is similar to an identifier reference for top-level bindings, except that *symbol* is evaluated by virtue of the fact that **top-level-value** is a procedure.

```
(begin
  (define-top-level-value 'xyz "hi")
  (top-level-value 'xyz))           ⇒ "hi"
(define xyz 3/4)
(let ([xyz "shadow"])
  (+ (top-level-value 'xyz)
     (top-level-value 'xyz)))       ⇒ 3/2
```

(set-top-level-value! *symbol obj*)   procedure

> returns: unspecified

set-top-level-value! is similar to a **set!** expression for top-level bindings, except that *symbol* is evaluated by virtue of the fact that **set-top-level-value!** is a procedure.

```
(begin
  (define-top-level-value 'xyz 3/4)
  (set-top-level-value! 'xyz (- 1 3/4))
  xyz)                                    ⇒ 1/4
```

(top-level-bound? *symbol*)   procedure

returns: #t if *symbol* is defined at toplevel, #f otherwise

This predicate is useful in an interpreter to check for the existence of a top-level binding, *e.g.*, before requesting the value with top-level-value.

```
(top-level-bound? 'xyz)         ⇒ #f
(define-top-level-value 'xyz 3)
(top-level-bound? 'xyz)         ⇒ #t
```

7-3 Cafés and Waiters

In *Chez* Scheme, the system interacts with the user through a program known as a *waiter*. A waiter is a Scheme program that cycles indefinitely, first prompting for input, then reading the next expression from the keyboard, then evaluating the expression, and finally printing the result. A waiter runs within the context of a *café*. The café defines a pair of procedures, reset and exit. Whenever it is invoked, reset terminates the current computation and returns to the waiter, and exit terminates the current computation and leaves the café. Typing the system-defined end-of-file (EOF) character in response to the waiter's prompt is equivalent to typing (exit).

It is possible to open up a chain of *Chez* Scheme cafés with the procedure new-cafe. Each café defines its own reset and exit procedures. Exiting from one café in the chain returns you to the next one back; exiting from the original café exits the system altogether. The procedure abort has the same effect as exiting from as many cafés as are currently active. It is often useful to interrupt the system (see Section 7–9), enter a new café to check the status of the system or to trace or untrace a procedure in the interrupted program (see trace), then exit the new café to continue the interrupted program.

(new-cafe)   procedure

    returns: unspecified

When the system starts up, you are automatically placed in a café and given a waiter to serve you. new-cafe opens a new Scheme café, stacked on top of the old one. In addition to starting the waiter, new-cafe sets up the café's reset and exit procedures. When you exit from a café, you return to the old café and continue from the call to new-cafe. When you exit from the initial café, you leave Scheme altogether.

(reset)   procedure

    returns: does not return

reset terminates the current computation, returns you to the current café, and restarts the waiter.

(exit)   procedure

    returns: does not return

exit exits from the current café (and from Scheme, if there is only one café).

(abort)   procedure

    returns: does not return

This exits from all levels of Scheme cafés, leaving Scheme altogether.

(waiter)   procedure

    returns: unspecified

waiter is invoked automatically by new-cafe each time you enter a new-cafe and each time you reset to the current café.

7-4 Transcript Files

A transcript file is a record of an interactive session. It is useful for creating an output file or listing of an interactive session or as a "quick-and-dirty" alternative to opening an output file and using explicit output operations.

(`transcript-on` *filename*)   procedure

(`transcript-off`)   procedure

> returns: unspecified

> *filename* must be a string.

> `transcript-on` opens the file named by *filename* for output, and it copies all input from the current input port and all output to the current output port to this file. An error is signaled if the file cannot be opened for output.

> `transcript-off` ends transcription and closes the transcript file.

> In *Chez* Scheme, `transcript-on` also enters a new café; exiting from this café (see `exit`) has the same effect as `transcript-off`.

7-5 Garbage Collection

Garbage collection is the automatic deallocation phase of the storage manager. Normally, it occurs whenever necessary to prevent the Scheme system from running out of storage space.

(`collect`)   procedure

> returns: unspecified

> `collect` causes the storage manager to perform a garbage collection. Any objects that the garbage collector proves can no longer be referenced are deallocated so that the storage space taken up by the objects can be reused. `collect` is normally invoked automatically by the Scheme system often enough to prevent the system from running out of storage, but in some circumstances it may be desirable to force collection at a particular time, *e.g.*, before timing a computation. If the identifier `*collect-notify*` is bound to a true value, `collect` prints a message whenever it is invoked, whether directly or automatically.

7-6 Statistics

(time *exp*)   syntax

   returns: value of *exp*

   time evaluates *exp* and, as a side-effect, prints the amount of cpu time,
   the amount of real time, the number of bytes allocated, and the amount
   of collection overhead associated with evaluating *exp*.

(display-statistics)   procedure

(display-statistics *output-port*)   procedure

   returns: unspecified

   If *output-port* is not supplied, it defaults to the current output port.

   display-statistics displays a running total of the amount of cpu time,
   real time, bytes allocated, and collection overhead.

(cpu-time)   procedure

   returns: the amount of cpu time consumed since system start-up

   The amount is in milliseconds.

(real-time)   procedure

   returns: the amount of real time that has elapsed since system start-up

   The amount is in milliseconds.

(bytes-allocated)   procedure

   returns: the total number of bytes currently allocated

(date-and-time)   procedure

   returns: a string giving the current date and time

7-7 Tracing

(trace-lambda *name idspec exp* ...)   syntax

> returns: a traced procedure

> This is equivalent to (lambda *idspec exp* ...) except that trace infor-
> mation is printed to the current output port whenever the procedure is
> invoked, using *name* to identify the procedure. The trace information
> shows the value of the arguments passed to the procedure and the value
> returned by the procedure, using indentation to show the nesting of calls.

(trace-let *name* ((*id val*) ...) *exp* ...)   syntax

> This is equivalent to (let *name* ((*id val*) ...) *exp* ...) except that
> trace information is printed to the current output port on entry to the
> let expression and each time *name* is invoked.

(trace *id* ...)   syntax

> returns: list of *id* ...

> This redefines the top-level value of the identifiers *id* ..., whose val-
> ues must be procedures, to trace calls to the procedures in a manner
> similar to trace-lambda. Only calls made through the identifier, *e.g.*,
> (*id arg* ...), are traced. Any current tracing of these procedures via a
> previous use of trace is turned off.

> trace with no arguments returns a list of the currently traced identifiers.

(untrace *id* ...)   syntax

> returns: list of *id* ...

> untrace restores the original (pre-trace) top-level value of the identifiers
> *id* ..., effectively discontinuing the tracing of calls made through the
> identifiers. If any of the identifiers has been rebound since it was traced,
> the old value is not restored. In either case, the *id* is removed from the
> set of traced objects.

> If untrace is called without arguments, all currently traced identifiers
> are untraced, and a list of these identifiers is returned.

7-8 Error Reporting and Handling

(error *symbol format-string obj* ...)   procedure

    returns: does not return

    error is used to report errors. *symbol* should identify the procedure or program that detects the error, and *format-string* should describe the error, including the remaining arguments *obj* ... as necessary in the manner of format.

    error is equivalent to (lambda args (apply *error-handler* args)).

```
(define repair
  (lambda (pair)
    (unless (pair? pair)
      (error 'repair "cannot repair non-pair ~s" pair))
    (cons (car pair) (cdr pair))))
```

    When passed a pair, repair returns a new, equivalent pair.

```
(repair '(a . b))  ⇒ (a . b)
```

    When passed something other than a pair, repair causes an error. For example,

```
(repair "not a pair")
```

    causes the error message

```
Error in repair: cannot repair non-pair "not a pair"
```

    to be reported.

(*error-handler* *symbol format-string obj* ...)   procedure

    returns: does not return

    The procedure bound to *error-handler* is invoked whenever an error is detected by the Scheme system or reported with error. By default, the error handler prints a message and resets to the current café, using *symbol* to identify the procedure that detected the error, and *format-string* and the remaining arguments to form the message (with format). It is possible to redefine *error-handler* to customize error handling for a particular application.

symbol may be (), in which case the procedure detecting the error is not identified. This is necessary because the system is sometimes unable to determine the name of the currently active procedure when it detects an error condition.

7-9 Exception Handling

Chez Scheme defines a set of primitive exception handlers that may be used to control the action of the Scheme system when various events occur, including an interrupt from the keyboard, a stack overflow, a request from the storage manager that a garbage collection be performed, or the expiration of an internal timer set by set-timer.

Most of these events occur asynchronously with respect to a particular computation, but they are treated as if they occurred synchronously with the first procedure call after the event occurs. For example, the user may type the system-defined interrupt key at any time during a computation, but the system does not respond to this interrupt until the next procedure call occurs.

When an exception condition is detected within the procedure call mechanism, the call is pended, or "put on hold," while the exception handler associated with the exception is invoked. When (if) the exception handler returns, the pending call takes place.

(*keyboard-interrupt-handler*)   procedure

   returns: unspecified

This is called by the system after a keyboard interrupt. The default handler prints an appropriate message and a menu of options. It is sometimes useful to redefine this procedure to customize keyboard interrupt handling to a particular application.

Some users prefer that the keyboard interrupt handler return to the current café and restart the waiter rather than prompting for options. This may be accomplished by setting *keyboard-interrupt-handler* to (lambda () (reset)).

(*stack-overflow-handler*)   procedure

  returns: unspecified

In *Chez* Scheme, the system stack (used to record procedure calls) is
automatically extended whenever the stack overflows. A stack overflow
usually, but not always, means that the current computation is stuck
in an infinite recursion; this handler exists so that the user may be
notified of the overflow. By default, the stack overflow handler prints an
appropriate message and a menu of options.

It is possible to redefine *stack-overflow-handler* to customize stack
overflow handling to a particular application. For example, it may
be desirable to ignore stack overflows during a computation that requires more stack space than the amount normally allocated to the
stack. This may be accomplished by setting *stack-overflow-handler*
to (lambda () #f).

(*collect-request-handler*)   procedure

  returns: unspecified

Whenever the storage allocator has allocated a given amount of storage (determined by the value of *collect-trip-bytes*), it requests that
a collection be performed at the first opportunity by causing a collect
request exception. By default, the collect request handler simply calls
collect. It may be useful to redefine this handler, say, to prevent collection during a section of code that is time-critical, since garbage collection
can sometimes take one second or more.

(*timer-interrupt-handler*)   procedure

This is called by the system when the internal timer (set by set-timer)
expires. The default handler signals an error to say that the handler has
not been defined; any program that uses the timer should redefine this
identifier before setting the timer.

The engine mechanism is built on top of the timer interrupt (see Section 9–7), so timer interrupts should not be used with engines.

(set-timer *ticks*)   procedure

  returns: current timer value

ticks must be a nonnegative integer.

With a nonzero argument, set-timer starts an internal timer with an initial value of *ticks*. When *ticks* virtual processing cycles elapse, a timer interrupt occurs, resulting in a call to *timer-interrupt-handler*. The amount of time corresponding to each *tick* is not specified and may be a function of the computation being performed. For example, the amount of time may be a function of the memory references or procedure calls performed by a computation, or of elapsed cpu time.

With an argument of 0, set-timer turns the timer off.

The value returned is the old value of the timer. Do not count on a return value of 0 to mean that the timer was not on. The return value may also be 0 if the timer was just about to fire when the call to set-timer occurred.

The engine mechanism is built on top of the timer interrupt (see Section 9–7), so timer interrupts should not be used with engines.

(disable-interrupts)   procedure

(enable-interrupts)   procedure

  returns: disable count

disable-interrupts disables the handling of the interrupts (and exceptions) described in this section. Calls to disable-interrupts are counted, and it takes as many calls to enable-interrupts as calls to disable-interrupts to cause interrupt handling to be enabled. For example, two calls to disable-interrupts followed by one call to enable-interrupts will leave interrupts disabled. The value returned by either procedure is the number of calls to enable-interrupts required to enable interrupts. This value is always nonnegative, *i.e.*, calls to enable-interrupts when interrupts are already enabled have no effect.

Great care should be exercised when using these procedures, since disabling interrupts defeats the normal processing of keyboard interrupts and, perhaps more importantly, requests for garbage collection. Since garbage collection does not happen automatically when interrupts are disabled, it is possible for the storage allocator to run out of space unnecessarily should interrupts be disabled for a long period of time.

Ordinarily, the `critical-section` special form should be used to disable interrupts, since it uses `dynamic-wind` to ensure that interrupts are reenabled in the case of an error.

`(critical-section exp ...)`   syntax

returns: result of last *exp*

`critical-section` evaluates the expressions in sequence (as if in a `begin`), without interruption. That is, upon entry to the critical section, interrupts are disabled, and upon exit, interrupts are reenabled. Thus, `critical-section` allows the implementation of indivisible operations.

`critical-section` may be defined as follows.

```
(extend-syntax (critical-section)
  [(critical-section exp ...)
   (dynamic-wind
      disable-interrupts
      (lambda () exp ...)
      enable-interrupts)])
```

The `dynamic-wind` ensures that interrupts will be disabled whenever the body of `critical-section` expression is active, and reenabled whenever it is not. Since calls to `disable-interrupts` are counted (see the discussion under `disable-interrupts` and `enable-interrupts` above), `critical-section` expressions may be nested with the desired effect.

Chapter 8: Syntactic Extension and Structures

The first section of this chapter describes the definition of syntactic extensions with `extend-syntax`. The second section describes the definition of new data structures with `define-structure`. The third section gives an implementation of `define-structure` that uses `extend-syntax`, providing at the same time an operational model for `define-structure` and a significant example of the power of `extend-syntax`.

Both `extend-syntax` and `define-structure` are specific to *Chez* Scheme, but similar mechanisms exist in most implementations of Scheme.

8-1 Syntactic Extension

This section describes `extend-syntax`, a powerful yet easy to use syntactic extension facility based on pattern matching [11]. `extend-syntax` automatically generates a syntactic transformation procedure for a given syntactic form from a set of pattern/expansion pairs that describes both the input to and the output from the transformation procedure. The syntactic transformation procedure is associated with the name, or syntax keyword, of the syntactic extension and is invoked by the system expander each time the syntactic extension appears in a source program to be evaluated (see **expand** in Section 7–1).

(extend-syntax (*name key* ...) (*pattern fender expansion*) ...)   syntax

returns: unspecified

The identifier *name* is the name, or syntax keyword, for the syntactic extension to be defined. When the system expander processes any list expression whose car is *name*, the syntactic transformation procedure generated by `extend-syntax` is invoked on this expression. The remaining identifiers *key* ... are additional keywords to be recognized within input expressions during expansion (such as `else` in `cond` or `case`).

Each clause after the list of keys consists of a *pattern*, an optional *fender*, and an *expansion*. The optional *fender* is omitted more often than not. The *pattern* specifies the syntax the input expression must have for the clause to be chosen. Identifiers within the pattern that are not keywords (*pattern variables*) are bound to corresponding pieces of the input expression. If present, the *fender* is a Scheme expression that specifies additional constraints on the input expression (accessed through the pattern variables) that must be satisified in order for the clause to be chosen. The *expansion* specifies what form the output takes, usually in terms of the pattern variables.

During expansion, the transformation procedure extend-syntax generates attempts to match the input expression against each pattern in the order the clauses are given. If the input expression matches the pattern, the pattern variables are bound to the corresponding pieces of the input expression and the fender for the clause, if any, is evaluated. If the fender returns a true value, the given expansion is performed. If input does not match the pattern or if the fender returns a false value, the tranformation procedure tries the next clause. An error is signaled if no clause can be chosen.

Within the pattern, ellipses (...) may be used to specify zero or more occurrences of the preceding pattern fragment, or prototype. Similarly, ellipses may be used in the output to specify the construction of zero or more expansion prototypes. In this case, the expansion prototype must contain part of an input pattern prototype. The use of patterns, expansions, ellipses within patterns and expansions, and fenders is illustrated in the following sequence of examples.

The first example, defining rec, uses a single keyword, a single clause with no fender, and no ellipses.

```
(extend-syntax (rec)
  [(rec id val)
   (let ([id #f])
     (set! id val)
     id)])
```

The procedure expand-once (Section 7–1) is useful for debugging syntactic extension definitions, expanding only one level.

```
(expand-once              (let ([eternal #f])
  '(rec eternal       ⇒     (set! eternal
     (lambda ()                (lambda ()
        (eternal))))             (eternal)))
                          eternal)
```

The second example, defining when, shows the use of ellipses.

```
(extend-syntax (when)
  [(when test exp1 exp2 ...)
   (if test (begin exp1 exp2 ...) #f)])
```

```
(expand-once              (if (eq? msg 'print)
  '(when (eq? msg 'print)  ⇒     (begin (display "hi")
     (display "hi")                  (newline))
     (newline)))          #f)
```

A next example shows the definition of let (from Section 2–10). The definition of let shows the use of multiple ellipses, employing one for the identifier/value pairs and one for the expressions in the body. It also shows that the prototype need not be a single identifier, and that pieces of the prototype may be separated from one another in the expansion.

```
(extend-syntax (let)
  [(let ([x v] ...) e1 e2 ...)
   ((lambda (x ...) e1 e2 ...) v ...)])
```

```
(expand-once              ((lambda (x y) (+ x y))
  '(let ([x 3] [y 4])   ⇒   3
     (+ x y)))              4)
```

The next example shows let*, whose syntax is the same as for let, but which is defined recursively in terms of let with two clauses (one for the base case, one for the recursion step) since it must produce a nested structure. (Recall from Section 2–4 that a let* expression is an abbreviation for nested let expressions.)

```
(extend-syntax (let*)
  [(let* () e1 e2 ...)
   (let () e1 e2 ...)]
  [(let* ([x v] more ...) e1 e2 ...)
   (let ([x v]) (let* (more ...) e1 e2 ...))])
```

The first pattern/expansion pair matches any let* expression with no identifier/value pairs and maps it into the equivalent begin expression. This is the base case. The second pattern/expansion pair matches any let* expression with one or more identifier/value pairs and transforms it into a let expression binding the first pair whose body is a let* expression binding the remaining pairs. This is the recursion step, which will eventually lead us to the base case because we remove one identifier/value pair at each step. Notice that the second pattern uses the pattern variable more for the second and later identifier/value pairs; this makes the pattern and expansion less cluttered and makes it clear that only the first identifier/value pair is dealt with explicitly.

It is interesting to try both expand-once and expand on a let* expression. expand-once shows the intermediate form in terms of let and a simpler let* expression; expand shows the expression completely expanded into applications of lambda expressions.

```
(expand-once                    (let ([x 3])
   '(let* ([x 3] [y x])  ⇒        (let* ([y x])
      (+ x y)))                       (+ x y)))
(expand                         ((lambda (x)
   '(let* ([x 3] [y x])  ⇒        ((lambda (y) (+ x y)) x))
      (+ x y)))                    3)
```

The definition for and requires three clauses. The first clause is necessary to recognize (and), and the second two define all other and forms recursively.

```
(extend-syntax (and)
   [(and) #t]
   [(and x) x]
   [(and x y ...) (if x (and y ...) #f)])
```

The definition for cond requires four clauses. As with let*, cond must be described recursively, partly because it produces nested if expressions, and partly because one ellipsis prototype would not be sufficient to describe all possible cond clauses. The definition of cond also requires that we specify else as a keyword, in addition to cond. Here is the definition:

```
(extend-syntax (cond else)
  [(cond) #f]
  [(cond (else e1 e2 ...))
   (begin e1 e2 ...)]
  [(cond (test) more ...)
   (or test (cond more ...))]
  [(cond (test e1 e2 ...) more ...)
   (if test
       (begin e1 e2 ...)
       (cond more ...))])
```

Two of the clauses are base cases and two are recursion steps. The first base case is an empty cond. The value of cond in this case is unspecified, so the choice of #f is somewhat arbitrary. The second base case is a cond containing only an else clause; this is transformed to the equivalent begin expression. The two recursion steps differ in the number of expressions in the cond clause. The value of cond when the first true clause contains only the test expression is the value of the test (see the definition of cond in Section 4-4). This is similar to what or does, so we expand the cond clause into an or expression. On the other hand, when there are expressions following the test expression, the value of the last expression is returned, so we use if and begin.

```
(expand-once                 (if test
  '(cond            ⇒            (begin exp1 exp2)
     [test exp1 exp2]))         (cond))
(expand-once
  '(cond [test]))   ⇒   (or test (cond))
(expand                      (if test1
  '(cond                        exp1
     [test1 exp1]     ⇒         (if test2
     [test2 exp2]                  exp2
     [else exp3]))                 exp3))
```

To be absolutely correct about the syntax of let, we actually must require that the bound identifiers in the input are symbols. If we typed something like (let ([3 x]) x) we would not get an error from let because it does not check to verify that the objects in the identifier positions are symbols. Instead, lambda may complain, or perhaps the system evaluator long after expansion is complete. This is where fenders are useful.

```
(extend-syntax (let)
   [(let ([x v] ...) e1 e2 ...)
    (andmap symbol? '(x ...))
    ((lambda (x ...) e1 e2 ...) v ...)])
```

The andmap of symbol? over '(x ...) assures that each bound identifier is a symbol. A fender is simply a Scheme expression. Within that expression, any quoted object is first expanded by the same rules as the expansion part of the clause. In this case, '(x ...) is expanded to the list of identifiers from the identifier/value pairs.

extend-syntax typically handles everything you need it for, but some syntactic extension definitions require the ability to include the result of evaluating an arbitrary Scheme expression. This ability is provided by with.

(with ((*pattern expression*) ...) *expansion*)   syntax

returns: processed *expansion*

with is valid only within an expansion inside of extend-syntax.

with patterns are the same as extend-syntax patterns, with expressions are the same as extend-syntax fenders, and with expansions are the same as extend-syntax expansions.

with can be used to introduce new pattern identifiers bound to expressions produced by arbitrary Scheme expressions within extend-syntax expansions. That is, with allows an escape from the declarative style of extend-syntax into the procedural style of full Scheme.

One common use of with is the introduction of a temporary identifier or list of temporary identifiers into an expansion. with is also used to perform complex transformations that might be clumsy or inefficient if performed within the extend-syntax framework.

For example, or requires the use of a temporary identifier. We could define or as follows.

```
(extend-syntax (or)
  [(or) #f]
  [(or x) x]
  [(or x y ...)
   (let ([temp x])
     (if temp temp (or y ...)))])
```

This would work until we placed an or expression within the scope of an occurrence of temp, in which case strange things could happen.

```
(let ([temp #t])
  (or #f temp))  ⇒ #f
```

One solution is to use gensym (see Section 5–7) and with to create a temporary identifier, as follows.

```
(extend-syntax (or)
  [(or) #f]
  [(or x) x]
  [(or x y ...)
   (with ([temp (gensym)])
     (let ([temp x])
       (if temp temp (or y ...))))])
```

Also, with can be used to combine elements of the input pattern in ways not possible directly with extend-syntax, such as the following folding-plus example.

```
(extend-syntax (folding-plus)
  [(folding-plus x y)
   (and (number? 'x) (number? 'y))
   (with ([val (+ 'x 'y)])
     val)]
  [(folding-plus x y) (+ x y)])
```

folding-plus collapses into the value of (+ x y) if both x and y are numeric constants. Otherwise, folding-plus is transformed into (+ x y) for later evaluation. The fender checks that the operands are numbers at expansion time, and the with performs the evaluation. As with fenders, expansion is performed only within a quoted expressions, since quote sets the data apart from the remainder of the Scheme expression.

```
(expand-once '(folding-plus 3 4.3))  ⇒ 7.3
(expand-once '(folding-plus 3 x))    ⇒ (+ 3 x)
```

In our final example, we bind a list of pattern variables to a list of temporary symbols, taking advantage of the fact that with allows us to bind patterns to expressions. This list of temporaries helps us to implement the sigma syntactic extension. sigma is similar to lambda, except it assigns the identifiers in the identifier list instead of creating new bindings. It may be used to perform a series of assignments in parallel.

```
(extend-syntax (sigma)
   [(sigma (x ...) e1 e2 ...)
    (with ([(t ...) (map (lambda (x) (gensym)) '(x ...))])
       (lambda (t ...)
          (set! x t) ...
          e1 e2 ...))])
```

```
(expand-once                         (lambda (G0 G1)
   '(sigma (x y)            ⇒           (set! x G0)
      (list x y)))                      (set! y G1)
                                        (list x y))
```

```
(let ([x 'a] [y 'b])
   ((sigma (x y) (list x y)) y x))  ⇒ (b a)
```

8-2 Structures

Chez Scheme supports the definition of new data structures, similar to Common Lisp structures, C structures, or Pascal records. Structure definition is straightforward. Each new structure created by define-structure has a constructor procedure, a type predicate, an access procedure for each of its fields, and an assignment procedure for each of its fields. define-structure allows the programmer to control which fields are arguments to the generated constructor procedure, and which fields are explicitly initialized by the constructor procedure.

define-structure is significantly less complex than structure facilities found in most Lisp dialects. However, it is powerful enough for most applications, and it is easily extended to handle applications for which it is not sufficient. In order to facilitate such extensions, the following section is devoted to a description of one possible implementation of define-structure with extend-syntax.

(define-structure (*name* id_1 ...) ((id_2 *val*) ...))   syntax
    returns: unspecified

> define-structure defines a new data structure, *name*, and creates a set of procedures for creating and manipulating instances of the structure. The identifiers id_1 ... and id_2 ... name the fields of the data structure.
>
> The following procedures are defined by define-structure:
>
> - a constructor procedure whose name is make-*name*,
>
> - a type predicate whose name is *name*?,
>
> - an access procedure whose name is *name-field* for each field name id_1 ... and id_2 ..., and
>
> - an assignment procedure whose name is set-*name-field*! for each field name id_1 ... and id_2 ....
>
> The fields named by the identifiers id_1 ... are initialized by the arguments to the constructor procedure. The fields named by the identifiers id_2 ... are initialized explicitly to the values of the expressions *val* .... These expressions are evaluated within the scope of the identifers id_1 ... (bound to the corresponding field value) and any of the identifiers id_2 ... (bound to the corresponding field value) appearing before it (as if within a let*).
>
> To clarify, the constructor behaves as if defined as
>
> ```
> (define make-name
>     (lambda (id_1 ...)
>         (let* ([id_2 val] ...)
>             ⟨body⟩))),
> ```
>
> where ⟨body⟩ builds the structure from the values of the identifiers id_1 ... and id_2 ....
>
> If no fields other than those initialized by the arguments to the constructor procedure are needed, the second subexpression, ((id_2 *val*) ...), may be omitted.
>
> The following simple example demonstrates how pairs might be defined in Scheme if they did not already exist. The only fields required are initialized by the arguments to the constructor procedure.

```
(define-structure (pare car cdr))
(define p (make-pare 'a 'b))
(pare? p)                                    ⇒ #t
(pair? p)                                    ⇒ #f
(pare? '(a . b))                             ⇒ #f
(pare-car p)                                 ⇒ a
(pare-cdr p)                                 ⇒ b
(set-pare-cdr! p (make-pare 'b 'c))
(pare-car (pare-cdr p))                      ⇒ b
(pare-cdr (pare-cdr p))                      ⇒ c
```

The following example defines a special string data structure, called a
stretch-string, that grows as needed. This example uses a field explicitly initialized to a value that depends on the value of the constructor
argument fields.

```
(define-structure (stretch-string length fill)
  ([string (make-string length fill)]))
(define stretch-string-ref
  (lambda (s i)
    (let ([n (stretch-string-length s)])
      (when (>= i n) (stretch-stretch-string! s (+ i 1) n))
      (string-ref (stretch-string-string s) i))))
(define stretch-string-set!
  (lambda (s i c)
    (let ([n (stretch-string-length s)])
      (when (>= i n) (stretch-stretch-string! s (+ i 1) n))
      (string-set! (stretch-string-string s) i c))))
(define stretch-string-fill!
  (lambda (s c)
    (string-fill! (stretch-string-string s) c)
    (set-stretch-string-fill! s c)))
(define stretch-stretch-string!
  (lambda (s i n)
    (set-stretch-string-length! s i)
    (let ([str (stretch-string-string s)]
          [fill (stretch-string-fill s)])
      (let ([xtra (make-string (- i n) fill)])
```

```
(set-stretch-string-string!
 s
 (string-append str xtra))))))
```

As it frequently happens, most of the procedures defined automatically are used only to define more specialized procedures, in this case the procedures stretch-string-ref and stretch-string-set!. The only automatically defined procedures that are likely to be useful in code using stretch strings are stretch-string-length and stretch-string-string.

```
(define ss (make-stretch-string 2 #\X))
(stretch-string-string ss)              ⇒ "XX"
(stretch-string-ref ss 3)               ⇒ #\X
(stretch-string-length ss)              ⇒ 4
(stretch-string-string ss)              ⇒ "XXXX"

(stretch-string-fill! ss #\@)
(stretch-string-string ss)              ⇒ "@@@@"
(stretch-string-ref ss 5)               ⇒ #\@
(stretch-string-string ss)              ⇒ "@@@@@@"

(stretch-string-set! ss 7 #\=)
(stretch-string-length ss)              ⇒ 8
(stretch-string-string ss)              ⇒ "@@@@@@@="
```

8-3 Implementation of Structures

This section describes one possible implementation of define-structure. It is defined entirely with extend-syntax, so it also serves as a practical and fairly complicated example of extend-syntax.

This version of define-structure implements structure instances as vectors, so it is not necessarily possible to tell the difference between a structure and a vector that looks like a structure. In the vector that implements a structure, the first element of the structure holds the name, or type, of that structure, and the generated type predicate for the structure is a three-part test: (1) make sure the object is a vector, (2) make sure it is of the expected length, and (3) check that its first element is the name of the structure. Although in theory this test could return true for an object that is not an instance of the structure in question, in practice it is quite sufficient.

The ambitious reader may wish to extend `define-structure` in one or more ways. For example, it might be useful to add an optional declaration of the form (`read-only` *id* ...) after the other subexpressions. `define-structure` would not create assignment procedures for the fields *id* .... Also, it might be useful to allow the type of object each field may hold to be declared in a similar manner. The constructor and assignment procedures would check the values assigned to these fields and signal an error if the value is not of the right type.

The definition of `define-structure` makes use of two pattern/expansion clauses. Two clauses are needed to handle the optionality of the second subexpression. The first clause matches the form without the second subexpression and merely converts it into the equivalent form with the second subexpression present, but empty.

The definition also makes heavy use of `with` to evaluate Scheme expressions at expansion time. The first four `with` clauses are used to manufacture the identifiers that name the automatically defined procedures. (The procedure `format` is particularly useful here, but it could be replaced with `string-append!`, using `symbol->string` as needed.) The first two clauses yield single identifiers (for the constructor and predicate), while the next two yield lists of identifiers (for the field access and assignment procedures). The fifth `with` clause (the final clause in the outer `with`) is used to count the total length vector needed for each instance of the structure, which must include room for the name and all of the fields. The final `with` clause (the only clause in the inner `with`) is used to create a list of vector indexes, one for each field (starting at 1, since the structure name occupies position 0).

```
(extend-syntax (define-structure)
  [(define-structure (name id1 ...))
   (define-structure (name id1 ...) ())]
  [(define-structure (name id1 ...) ([id2 val] ...))
   (with ([constructor
            (string->symbol (format "make-~a" 'name))]
          [predicate
            (string->symbol (format "~a?" 'name))]
          [(access ...)
           (map (lambda (x)
                  (string->symbol
                    (format "~a-~a" 'name x)))
                '(id1 ... id2 ...))]
          [(assign ...)
```

```scheme
              (map (lambda (x)
                     (string->symbol
                       (format "set-~a-~a!" 'name x)))
                   '(id1 ... id2 ...))]
         [count (length '(name id1 ... id2 ...))])
    (with ([(index ...)
             (let f ([i 1])
               (if (= i 'count)
                   '()
                   (cons i (f (+ i 1)))))])
      (begin
        (define constructor
          (lambda (id1 ...)
            (let* ([id2 val] ...)
              (vector 'name id1 ... id2 ...))))
        (define predicate
          (lambda (obj)
            (and (vector? obj)
                 (= (vector-length obj) count)
                 (eq? (vector-ref obj 0) 'name))))
        (define access
          (lambda (obj)
            (vector-ref obj index)))
        ...
        (define assign
          (lambda (obj newval)
            (vector-set! obj index newval)))
        ...)))])
```

The code below shows the set of procedures defined by this implementation of define-structure for the stretch-string structure shown in the previous section, obtained with expand-once:

```scheme
(expand-once
  '(define-structure (stretch-string length fill)
     ([string (make-string length fill)])))
```

⇒

```
(begin
  (define make-stretch-string
    (lambda (length fill)
      (let* ([string (make-string length fill)])
        (vector 'stretch-string length fill string))))
  (define stretch-string?
    (lambda (obj)
      (and (vector? obj)
           (= (vector-length obj) 4)
           (eq? (vector-ref obj 0) 'stretch-string))))
  (define stretch-string-length
    (lambda (obj)
      (vector-ref obj 1)))
  (define stretch-string-fill
    (lambda (obj)
      (vector-ref obj 2)))
  (define stretch-string-string
    (lambda (obj)
      (vector-ref obj 3)))
  (define set-stretch-string-length!
    (lambda (obj val)
      (vector-set! obj 1 val)))
  (define set-stretch-string-fill!
    (lambda (obj val)
      (vector-set! obj 2 val)))
  (define set-stretch-string-string!
    (lambda (obj val)
      (vector-set! obj 3 val))))
```

Chapter 9: Extended Examples

This chapter gives some examples of Scheme programs or useful packages that perform more complex tasks than most of the simpler examples found throughout the earlier chapters of the book. The programs serve to illustrate a variety of programming techniques and demonstrate a particular Scheme programming style.

Each section of this chapter describes one program in detail. The program to be displayed is first described along with examples of its use. This is followed by a listing of the code. At the end of each section are exercises intended to stimulate thought about the program and to suggest possible extensions. These exercises are generally more difficult than those found in Chapter 2.

Each example illustrates a different set of programming abstractions. The first and most basic is a matrix/vector/scalar multiplication package. It demonstrates a set of procedures that could be written in almost any language. Its most interesting feature is that all multiplication operations are performed by calling a single *generic* procedure, mul, that calls the appropriate help procedure depending upon the types of its arguments.

The second example is a word counting program borrowed from *The C Programming Language* [9], translated from C into Scheme. It shows character and string manipulation, structure creation and use, and basic file input and output.

The next example, a simple interpreter for Scheme, illustrates Scheme as a language implementation vehicle, giving as well an operational semantics for Scheme itself (and a useful basis for extensions to Scheme).

The fourth example defines a syntactic form that is used to construct sets. It demonstrates a simple but efficient syntactic transformation from set notation into Scheme code.

A small abstract object facility is next, illustrating another use for syntactic extensions and giving a useful basis for an entire object-oriented subsystem.

Sixth is a concise unification algorithm showing how procedures can be used as continuations and as substitutions (unifiers) in Scheme.

The seventh and final example shows the implementation of engines in terms of continuations and timer interrupts.

9-1 Matrix and Vector Multiplication

This example program involves mostly basic programming techniques. It demonstrates simple arithmetic and vector operations, looping with the do syntactic form, dispatching based on object type, and generating error messages.

Multiplication of scalar to scalar, scalar to vector, scalar to matrix, vector to vector, vector to matrix, and matrix to matrix is performed by a single *generic* procedure, called mul. Because scalar multiplication uses Scheme's multiplication procedure, *, mul scalars can be any built-in numeric type (complex, real, rational, or integer).

The product of an $m \times n$ matrix A and an $n \times p$ matrix B is the $m \times p$ matrix C whose entries are defined by

$$C_{ij} = \sum_{k=0}^{n-1} A_{ik} B_{kj}.$$

Vector-vector, vector-matrix, and matrix-vector multiplication may be considered special cases of matrix-matrix multiplication, where a vector is treated as a $1 \times n$ or $n \times 1$ matrix depending upon the context. To be precise, the product of two length n vectors U and V is the length n vector W whose entries are defined by

$$W_i = U_i V_i;$$

the product of an $m \times n$ matrix A and a length n vector V is the length n vector W whose entries are defined by

$$W_i = \sum_{k=0}^{n-1} A_{ik} V_k;$$

and the product of a length n vector U and an $n \times p$ matrix B is the length n vector W whose entries are defined by

$$W_j = \sum_{k=0}^{n-1} U_k B_{kj}.$$

The product of a scalar x and an $m \times n$ matrix A is the $m \times n$ matrix C whose entries are defined by the equation:

$$C_{ij} = x A_{ij}.$$

That is, each element of C is the product of x and the corresponding element of A. The product of a scalar x and a length n vector U is the length n vector W whose entries are defined by the equation:

$$W_i = xU_i.$$

The structure of the code is worth explaining briefly. The first few definitions establish a set of procedures that support the matrix datatype. A matrix is a vector of vectors. Included are a procedure to create matrices, procedures to access and assign matrix elements, and a matrix predicate. Inside the letrec expression that follows these definitions are a set of help procedures to support mul. The definition for mul to the value #f outside of the letrec expression establishes the top-level binding for mul, while the assignment to mul within the letrec expression gives mul its value. If the definition for mul were placed inside of the letrec, it would be local to the letrec and hence not visible outside (see define in Section 3–3).

The generic procedure mul checks the type of its arguments and chooses the appropriate help procedure to do the work. Each of these help procedures operates on arguments of specific types. For example, vec-sca-mul multiplies a vector by a scalar. If the type of either argument is invalid, or if the arguments are incompatible, e.g., rows or columns do not match up, mul or one of the help procedures signals an error.

mul is called with two arguments. Here are some examples showing the possible combinations, each preceded by the equivalent operation in standard mathematical notation.

- Scalar times scalar:
$$3 \times 4 = 12$$

(mul 3 4) $\Rightarrow$ 7

- Scalar times vector:
$$1/2 \times (1 \quad 2 \quad 3) = (1/2 \quad 1 \quad 3/2)$$

(mul 1/2 #(1 2 3)) $\Rightarrow$ #(1/2 1 3/2)

- Scalar times matrix:
$$-2 \times \begin{pmatrix} 3 & -2 & -1 \\ -3 & 0 & -5 \\ 7 & -1 & -1 \end{pmatrix} = \begin{pmatrix} -6 & 4 & 2 \\ 6 & 0 & 10 \\ -14 & 2 & 2 \end{pmatrix}$$

```
(mul -2
    #(#(3 -2 -1)      ⇒ #(#(-6 4 2)
      #(-3 0 -5)           #(6 0 10)
      #(7 -1 -1)))          #(-14 2 2))
```

- Vector times vector:

$$(1.1 \quad 2) \times (-4 \quad 5/3) = (-4.4 \quad 10/3)$$

```
(mul #(1.1 2) #(-4 5/3))  ⇒ #(-4.4 10/3)
```

- Vector times matrix:

$$(1 \quad 2 \quad 3) \times \begin{pmatrix} 2 & 3 \\ 3 & 4 \\ 4 & 5 \end{pmatrix} = \begin{pmatrix} 20 \\ 26 \end{pmatrix}$$

```
(mul #(1 2 3)
     #(#(2 3)      ⇒ #(20 26)
       #(3 4)
       #(4 5)))
```

- Matrix times vector:

$$\begin{pmatrix} 2 & 3 & 4 \\ 3 & 4 & 5 \end{pmatrix} \times \begin{pmatrix} 1 \\ 2 \\ 3 \end{pmatrix} = (20 \quad 26)$$

```
(mul #(#(2 3 4)
       #(3 4 5))  ⇒ #(20 26)
     #(1 2 3))
```

- Matrix times matrix:

$$\begin{pmatrix} 1 & 2 & 3 \\ 4 & 5 & 6 \end{pmatrix} \times \begin{pmatrix} 1 & 2 & 3 & 4 \\ 2 & 3 & 4 & 5 \\ 3 & 4 & 5 & 6 \end{pmatrix} = \begin{pmatrix} 14 & 20 & 26 & 32 \\ 32 & 47 & 62 & 77 \end{pmatrix}$$

```
(mul #(#(1 2 3)
       #(4 5 6))
     #(#(1 2 3 4)    ⇒ #(#(14 20 26 32)
       #(2 3 4 5)         #(32 47 62 77))
       #(3 4 5 6)))
```

Here is the code. Exercises appear after the code at the end of the section.

```
;;; make-matrix creates a matrix (a vector of vectors)
(define make-matrix
   (lambda (rows columns)
      (do ([m (make-vector rows)]
            [i 0 (1+ i)])
          ((= i rows) m)
          (vector-set! m i (make-vector columns)))))
;;; matrix? checks to see if its argument is a matrix.
;;; It isn't foolproof, but it's generally good enough
(define matrix?
   (lambda (x)
      (and (vector? x)
            (> (vector-length x) 0)
            (vector? (vector-ref x 0)))))
;;; matrix-ref returns the jth element of the ith row.
(define matrix-ref
   (lambda (m i j)
      (vector-ref (vector-ref m i) j)))
;;; matrix-set! changes the jth element of the ith row.
(define matrix-set!
   (lambda (m i j x)
      (vector-set! (vector-ref m i) j x)))
;;; mul is given its value in the body of the letrec
(define mul #f)
(letrec
   ;; type-error is called to complain when mul receives an invalid
   ;; type of argument.
   ([type-error
      (lambda (what)
         (error 'mul
            "~s is not a number, vector or matrix"
            what))]
   ;; match-error is called to complain when mul receives a pair of
   ;; incompatible arguments.
   [match-error
      (lambda (what1 what2)
         (error 'mul
```

```
                  "~s and ~s are incompatible operands"
                  what1
                  what2))]
;; matrix-rows returns the number of rows in a matrix.
[matrix-rows
   (lambda (x)
      (vector-length x))]
;; matrix-columns returns the number of columns in a matrix.
[matrix-columns
   (lambda (x)
      (vector-length (vector-ref x 0)))]
;; vec-sca-mul multiplies a vector by a scalar.
[vec-sca-mul
   (lambda (v x)
      (let* ([n (vector-length v)]
             [r (make-vector n)])
         (do ([i 0 (1+ i)])
             ((= i n) r)
             (vector-set! r i
                (* (vector-ref v i) x)))))]
;; vec-vec-mul multiplies two vectors, after verifying that the
;; vectors have the same length.
[vec-vec-mul
   (lambda (v1 v2)
      (let* ([n1 (vector-length v1)]
             [r (make-vector n1)])
         (unless (= (vector-length v2) n1)
            (match-error v1 v2))
         (do ([i 0 (1+ i)])
             ((= i n1) r)
             (vector-set! r i
                (* (vector-ref v1 i)
                   (vector-ref v2 i))))))]
;; mat-sca-mul multiplies a matrix by a scalar.
[mat-sca-mul
   (lambda (m x)
      (let* ([nr (matrix-rows m)]
             [nc (matrix-columns m)]
             [r  (make-matrix nr nc)])
```

```
         (do ([i 0 (1+ i)])
             ((= i nr) r)
             (do ([j 0 (1+ j)])
                 ((= j nc))
                 (matrix-set! r i j
                    (* x (matrix-ref m i j)))))))))]
;; vec-mat-mul multiplies a vector by a matrix, after verifying
;; that the vector has as many elements as matrix has rows.
[vec-mat-mul
   (lambda (v m)
      (let* ([nr (matrix-rows m)]
             [nc (matrix-columns m)]
             [r  (make-vector nc)])
         (unless (= (vector-length v) nr)
            (match-error v m))
         (do ([i 0 (1+ i)])
             ((= i nc) r)
             (do ([j 0 (1+ j)]
                  [a 0
                     (+ a
                        (* (matrix-ref m j i)
                           (vector-ref v j)))])
                 ((= j nr) (vector-set! r i a)))))))]
;; mat-vec-mul multiplies a matrix by a vector, after verifying
;; that the matrix has as many columns as vector has elements.
[mat-vec-mul
   (lambda (m v)
      (let* ([nr (matrix-rows m)]
             [nc (matrix-columns m)]
             [r  (make-vector nr)])
         (unless (= (vector-length v) nc)
            (match-error m v))
         (do ([i 0 (1+ i)])
             ((= i nr) r)
             (do ([j 0 (1+ j)]
                  [a 0
                     (+ a
                        (* (matrix-ref m i j)
                           (vector-ref v j)))])
```

```scheme
                ((= j nc) (vector-set! r i a))))))]
;; mat-mat-mul multiplies one matrix by another, after verifying
;; that the first matrix has as many columns as the second
;; matrix has rows.
[mat-mat-mul
   (lambda (m1 m2)
      (let* ([nr1 (matrix-rows m1)]
             [nr2 (matrix-rows m2)]
             [nc2 (matrix-columns m2)]
             [r   (make-matrix nr1 nc2)])
         (unless (= (matrix-columns m1) nr2)
            (match-error m1 m2))
         (do ([i 0 (1+ i)])
             ((= i nr1) r)
            (do ([j 0 (1+ j)])
                ((= j nc2))
               (do ([k 0 (1+ k)]
                    [a 0
                       (+ a
                          (* (matrix-ref m1 i k)
                             (matrix-ref m2 k j)))])
                   ((= k nr2)
                    (matrix-set! r i j a)))))))]
;; the generic matrix/vector/scalar multiplication procedure
(set! mul
   (lambda (x y)
      (cond
         [(matrix? x)
          (cond
             [(matrix? y) (mat-mat-mul x y)]
             [(vector? y) (mat-vec-mul x y)]
             [(number? y) (mat-sca-mul x y)]
             [else (type-error y)])]
         [(vector? x)
          (cond
             [(matrix? y) (vec-mat-mul x y)]
             [(vector? y) (vec-vec-mul x y)]
             [(number? y) (vec-sca-mul x y)]
             [else (type-error y)])]
```

```
        [(number? x)
         (cond
            [(matrix? y) (mat-sca-mul y x)]
            [(vector? y) (vec-sca-mul y x)]
            [(number? y) (* x y)]
            [else (type-error y)])]
        [else (type-error x)]))))
```

Exercise 9–1: Make the necessary changes to rename mul to *.

Exercise 9–2: The predicate matrix? is usually sufficient but not completely reliable, since it may return #t for objects that are not matrices. In particular, it does not verify that all of the matrix rows are vectors, that each row has the same number of elements, or that the elements themselves are numbers. Modify matrix? to perform each of these additional checks. It would be most appropriate to define a new predicate, number-vector?, that returns #t if its argument is a vector of numbers. This procedure could be used within matrix? and also within the body of mul in place of the less appropriate vector? test.

Exercise 9–3: Write similar generic procedures for addition and subtraction. Devise a generic dispatch procedure or syntactic form so that the type dispatching code need not be rewritten for each new operation.

Exercise 9–4: It seems as if we are duplicating code by not using vec-vec-mul in the definition of mat-vec-mul, vec-mat-mul, and mat-mat-mul. Redesign the system to avoid the duplication of code.

Exercise 9–5: This version of mul uses vectors to represent vectors and vectors of vectors to represent matrices. Rewrite the system using lists and nested lists to represent vectors and matrices. What efficiency is gained or lost by this change?

9-2 Word Frequency Counting

This program demonstrates several basic programming techniques including string and character manipulation, file input/output, structure creation and access, and recursion. As was mentioned in the introduction to this chapter, it is adapted from Chapter 6 of *The C Programming Language* [9]. One reason for using this particular example is to show how a C program might look when converted almost literally into Scheme.

A few differences between the Scheme program and the original C program are worth noting. First, the Scheme version employs a different protocol for file input and output. Rather than implicitly use the standard input and output ports, it requires that filenames be passed in, thus demonstrating the opening and closing of files. Second, the procedure get-word returns one of three values: a string (the word), a nonalphabetic character, or an eof value. The original C version returned a flag for letter (to say that a word was read) or a nonalphabetic character. Furthermore, the C version passed in a string to fill and a limit on the number of characters in the string; the Scheme version builds a new string of whatever length is required (the characters in the word are held in a list until the end of the word has been found, then converted into a string with list->string). Finally, char-type uses the primitive Scheme character predicates char-alphabetic? and char-numeric? to determine whether a character is a letter or digit.

The main program, frequency, takes an input filename and an output filename as arguments, e.g., (frequency "pickle" "freq.out") prints the frequency count for each word on the file "pickle" onto the file "freq.out". As frequency reads words from the input file, it inserts them into a binary tree structure (using a binary sorting algorithm). Duplicate entries are recorded by incrementing the count associated with each word. Once end of file is reached, the program traverses the tree, printing each word with its count.

Assume that the file "pickle" contains the following text.

```
Peter Piper picked a peck of pickled peppers;
A peck of pickled peppers Peter Piper picked.
If Peter Piper picked a peck of pickled peppers,
Where's the peck of pickled peppers Peter Piper picked?
```

Then, after typing (frequency "pickle" "freq.out"), the file "freq.out" should contain the following.

```
1 A
1 If
4 Peter
4 Piper
1 Where
2 a
4 of
```

```
4 peck
4 peppers
4 picked
4 pickled
1 s
1 the
```

(On some systems, the capitalized words may appear after the others.)
Here is the code.

```
;;; If the next character on p is a letter, get-word reads a word
;;; from p and returns it in a string.  If the character is not a
;;; letter, get-word returns the character (on eof, the eof-object).
(define get-word
   (lambda (p)
      (let ([c (read-char p)])
         (if (eq? (char-type c) 'letter)
             (list->string
                (let loop ([c c])
                   (if (memq (char-type c) '(letter digit))
                       (cons c (loop (read-char p)))
                       (begin
                          (unread-char c p)
                          '()))))
             c))))
;;; char-type tests for the eof-object first, since the eof-object
;;; may not be a valid argument to char-alphabetic? or char-numeric?
;;; It returns the eof-object, the symbol letter, the symbol digit,
;;; or the argument  itself if it is not a letter or digit.
(define char-type
   (lambda (c)
      (cond
         [(eof-object? c) c]
         [(char-alphabetic? c) 'letter]
         [(char-numeric? c) 'digit]
         [else c])))
;;; The tree structure has four fields.  Only one field, tree-word,
;;; is initialized by an argument to the constructor procedure
;;; make-tree.  The remaining fields are explicitly initialized and
;;; changed by subsequent operations.
```

```scheme
.efine-structure (tree word)
  ([left '()] [right '()] [count 1]))
;;; If the word already exists in the tree, tree increments its
;;; count.  Otherwise, a new tree node is created and put into the
;;; tree.  In any case, the new or modified tree is returned.
(define tree
   (lambda (node word)
      (cond
         [(null? node) (make-tree word)]
         [(string=? word (tree-word node))
          (set-tree-count! node (+ (tree-count node) 1))
          node]
         [(string<? word (tree-word node))
          (set-tree-left! node (tree (tree-left node) word))
          node]
         [else
          (set-tree-right! node (tree (tree-right node) word))
          node]])))
;;; tree-print prints the tree in "in-order," i.e., left subtree,
;;; then node, then right subtree.  For each word, the count and the
;;; word are printed on a single line.
(define tree-print
   (lambda (node p)
      (unless (null? node)
         (tree-print (tree-left node) p)
         (fprintf p "~a ~a~%"
            (tree-count node)
            (tree-word node))
         (tree-print (tree-right node) p))))
;;; frequency is the driver routine.  It opens the files, reads the
;;; words, and enters them into the tree.  When the input port
;;; reaches end-of-file, it prints the tree and closes the ports.
(define frequency
   (lambda (infn outfn)
      (let ([ip (open-input-file infn)]
            [op (open-output-file outfn)])
         (let loop ([root '()])
            (let ([w (get-word ip)])
               (cond
```

```
               [(eof-object? w) (tree-print root op)]
               [(string? w) (loop (tree root w))]
               [else (loop root)]])))
      (close-input-port ip)
      (close-output-port op))))
```

Exercise 9–6: In the output file shown earlier, the capitalized words appeared before the others in the output file, and the capital A was not recogized as the same word as the lower-case a. Modify tree to use the case-insensitive versions of the string comparisons so that this does not happen.

Exercise 9–7: The "word" s appeared in the file "freq.out", although it is really just a part of the contraction Where's. Adjust get-word to allow embedded single quote marks.

Exercise 9–8: Modify this program to "weed out" certain common words such as a, an, the, is, of, *etc.*in order to reduce the amount of output for long input files. Try to devise other ways to cut down on useless output.

Exercise 9–9: get-word buffers characters in a list, allocating a new pair (with cons) for each character. Make it more efficient by using a string to buffer the characters. Devise a way to allow the string to grow if necessary. [*Hint:* Use string-append (see stretch-string in Section 8–2).]

Exercise 9–10: This tree algorithm works by creating trees and later filling in its left and right fields. This requires many unnecessary assignments. Rewrite the tree procedure to avoid set-tree-left! and set-tree-right! entirely.

9-3 A Meta-Circular Interpreter for Scheme

This program is a *meta-circular* interpreter for Scheme, because it is an interpreter *for* Scheme written *in* Scheme. The interpreter shows how small Scheme really is, when the basic structure is considered independently from its syntactic extensions and primitives. It also illustrates interpretation techniques that can be applied equally well to languages other than Scheme.

The relative simplicity of the interpreter is somewhat misleading. An interpreter for Scheme written in Scheme is quite a bit simpler than it would be if written in most other languages. Here are a few reasons why:

- Tail calls are optimized only because tail recursion in the interpreter is optimized by the host system. All that is required is that the interpreter itself be tail recursive.
- First-class continuations created with call/cc are provided by the host system's call/cc.
- First-class procedures in interpreted code are implemented by first-class procedures in the interpreter, which in turn are supported by the host system.
- Primitive procedures such as car and read and services such as storage management are provided by the host system.

Converting the interpreter to run in a language other than Scheme may require explicit support for some or perhaps all of these items.

The interpreter stores lexical bindings in an *environment*, which is simply an *association list* (see assq). Evaluation of a lambda expression results in the creation of a procedure over the environment and the lambda body. Subsequent application of the procedure combines the new bindings (the actual parameters) with the saved environment.

Evaluation with interpret should yield the expected results:

```
(interpret 3)           ⇒ 3
(interpret '(+ 3 4))    ⇒ 7
(interpret
   '(let ([x 3] [y 4])
      (+ x y)))         ⇒ 7

(define fact
   (interpret
      (lambda (x)
         (if (zero? x)
             1
             (* x (fact (1- x)))))))
(fact 10)                              ⇒ 3628800
```

Here is the code:

```
;;; interpret is given its value in the body of the letrec
(define interpret #f)
(letrec
    ;; new-env returns a new environment from an identifier list, a
    ;; list of values, and an outer environment.  The symbol? test
    ;; checks for "improper" argument lists.  Environments are
```

```
;; association lists, associating identifiers with values.
([new-env
    (lambda (idl vals env)
       (cond
          [(null? idl) env]
          [(symbol? idl) (cons (cons idl vals) env)]
          [else
           (cons (cons (car idl) (car vals))
                 (new-env (cdr idl) (cdr vals) env))]))]
;; lookup looks for the identifier in env first, using assq.  If
;; it is not found, lookup returns the top-level binding.
[lookup
    (lambda (id env)
       (let ([pair (assq id env)])
          (if (null? pair)
              (top-level-value id)
              (cdr pair))))]
;; assign is similar to lookup, but alters the association pair
;; or the top-level-binding.
[assign
    (lambda (id val env)
       (let ([pair (assq id env)])
          (if (null? pair)
              (set-top-level-value! id val)
              (set-cdr! pair val))))]
;; exec evaluates the expression, recognizing all core forms.
[exec
    (lambda (exp env)
       (cond
          [(symbol? exp) (lookup exp env)]
          [(pair? exp)
           (case (car exp)
              [quote (cadr exp)]
              [lambda
               (lambda vals
                  ; make the begin case handle the implicit begin
                  (exec (cons 'begin (cddr exp))
                        (new-env (cadr exp) vals env)))]
              [if
```

```
                          (if (exec (cadr exp) env)
                              (exec (caddr exp) env)
                              (exec (cadddr exp) env))]
                      [set!
                       (assign (cadr exp)
                               (exec (caddr exp) env)
                               env)]
                      [begin
                       (let loop ([exps (cdr exp)])
                          (if (null? (cdr exps))
                              (exec (car exps) env)
                              (begin
                                  (exec (car exps) env)
                                  (loop (cdr exps)))))]
                      [else
                       (apply (exec (car exp) env)
                              (map (lambda (x) (exec x env))
                                   (cdr exp)))])]
                 [else exp])])))
;; interpret calls expand to expand syntactic extensions, then
;; calls exec on the result with an empty environment.
(set! interpret
   (lambda (exp)
      (exec (expand exp) '())))))
```

Exercise 9–11: It is possible to use the interpreter to interpret itself (that is, to evaluate the same code). What characteristics of the interpreter (or Scheme) make this possible? Use the interpreter to run a copy of itself, and the copy to run another copy. Repeat this process to see how many levels deep it will go before the Scheme system grinds to a halt.

Exercise 9–12: At first glance, it might seem that the begin case could be written more simply as follows:

```
[begin
 (let loop ([exps (cdr exp)])
    (let ([val (exec (car exps) env)])
       (if (null? (cdr exps))
           val
           (loop (cdr exps)))))]
```

Why would this be incorrect? [*Hint:* What property of Scheme would be violated?]

Exercise 9–13: Try to make the interpreter more efficient by looking for ways to ask fewer questions or allocate less storage space. [*Hint:* Before evaluation, convert lexical variable references into (access *n*), where *n* represents the number of values in the environment association list in front of the value in question.]

Exercise 9–14: Scheme evaluates arguments to a procedure before applying the procedure, applying the procedure to the values of these arguments (*call-by-value*). Modify the interpreter to pass arguments unevaluated and arrange to evaluate them upon reference (*call-by-name*). [*Hint:* Use lambda to delay evaluation.] You will need to create a library of primitive procedures (car, null?, *etc.*) that take their arguments unevaluated.

9-4 A Set Constructor

This example describes a syntactic extension, set-of, that allows the construction of sets represented as lists with no repeated elements [14]. It illustrates a relatively complex use of extend-syntax, requiring the compilation of set expressions into recursion expressions. The code produced is often as efficient as that which can be produced by hand.

set-of takes the form

   (set-of *value exp* ...).

value describes the elements of the set in terms of the bindings established by the expressions *exp* .... Each of the expressions *exp* ... can take one of three forms.

1 An expression of the form (*x* in *s*) establishes a binding for *x* to each element of the set *s* in turn. This binding is visible within the remaining expressions *exp* ... and the value *value*.

2 An expression of the form (*x* is *e*) establishes a binding for *x* to *e*. This binding is visible within the remaining expressions *exp* ... and the value *value*. This form is essentially an abbreviation for (*x* in (list *e*)).

3 An expression taking any other form is treated as a predicate; this is used to force refusal of certain elements as in the second of the three examples below.

```
(set-of x
    (x in '(a b c)))    ⇒ (a b c)
(set-of x
    (x in '(1 2 3 4))   ⇒ (2 4)
    (even? x))
(set-of (cons x y)
    (x in '(1 2 3))     ⇒ ((1 . 1) (2 . 4) (3 . 9))
    (y is (* x x)))
(set-of (cons x y)
    (x in '(a b))       ⇒ ((a . 1) (a . 2) (b . 1) (b . 2))
    (y in '(1 2)))
```

A set-of expression is transformed into nested let, named let, and if expressions, corresponding to each is, in, or predicate subexpression. For example, the simple expression

```
(set-of x (x in '(a b c)))
```

would be transformed into

```
(let loop ([set '(a b c)])
    (if (null? set)
        '()
        (let ([x (car set)])
            (set-cons x (loop (cdr set)))))).
```

The expression

```
(set-of x (x in '(1 2 3 4)) (even? x))
```

would be transformed into

```
(let loop ([set '(1 2 3 4)])
    (if (null? set)
        '()
        (let ([x (car set)])
            (if (even? x)
                (set-cons x (loop (cdr set)))
                (loop (cdr set)))))).
```

The more complicated expression

```
(set-of (cons x y) (x in '(1 2 3)) (y is (* x x)))
```

would be transformed into

```
(let loop ([set '(1 2 3)])
  (if (null? set)
      '()
      (let ([x (car set)])
        (let ([y (* x x)])
          (set-cons (cons x y)
                    (loop (cdr set)))))))))
```

Finally, the expression

```
(set-of (cons x y) (x in '(a b)) (y in '(1 2)))
```

would be transformed into nested named let expressions:

```
(let loop1 ([set1 '(a b)])
  (if (null? set1)
      '()
      (let ([x (car set1)])
        (let loop2 ([set2 '(1 2)])
          (if (null? set2)
              (loop1 (cdr set1))
              (let ([y (car set2)])
                (set-cons (cons x y)
                          (loop2 (cdr set2))))))))))).
```

These are fairly straightforward transformations, except that the base case for the recursion on nested named let expressions varies depending upon the level. The base case for the outermost named let is always the empty list (), while the base case for an internal named let is the recursion step for the next outer named let. In order to handle this, the definition of set-of employs a help syntactic extension set-of-help. set-of-help takes an additional expression, base, which is the base case for recursion at the current level.

Here is the code.

```
;;; set-of uses helper syntactic extension set-of-help, passing it
;;; an initial base expression of '()
(extend-syntax (set-of)
  [(set-of e m ...)
   (set-of-help e '() m ...)])
;;; set-of-help recognizes in, is and predicate expressions and
;;; changes them into nested named let, let, and if expressions.  In
```

```
;;; the case of named let expressions, two unique identifiers, loop
;;; and set, are created for each loop with gensym to avoid clashes
;;; among themselves and within the user's code.
(extend-syntax (set-of-help in is)
   [(set-of-help e base)
    (set-cons e base)]
   [(set-of-help e base (x in s) m ...)
    (with ([loop (gensym)] [set (gensym)])
       (let loop ([set s])
          (if (null? set)
              base
              (let ([x (car set)])
                 (set-of-help e (loop (cdr set)) m ...))))))]
   [(set-of-help e base (x is y) m ...)
    (let ([x y]) (set-of-help e base m ...))]
   [(set-of-help e base p m ...)
    (if p (set-of-help e base m ...) base)])
;;; set-cons uses memv, which is based on eqv?, to avoid potential
;;; problems with memq (eq?) on numbers and characters
(define set-cons
   (lambda (x y)
      (if (memv x y)
          y
          (cons x y))))
```

Exercise 9–15: Write a procedure, union, that takes an arbitrary number of sets (lists) as arguments and returns the union of the sets, using only the set-of syntactic form. For example:

(union)	⇒ ()
(union '(a b c))	⇒ (a b c)
(union '(2 5 4) '(9 4 3))	⇒ (2 5 9 4 3)
(union '(1 2) '(2 4) '(4 8))	⇒ (1 2 4 8)

Exercise 9–16: A single-list version of map can (almost) be defined as follows:

```
(define map1
  (lambda (f ls)
    (set-of (f x) (x in ls))))
(map1 1+ '(1 2 3 2))                    ⇒ (2 3 4)
```

Why does this not work? What could be changed to make it work?

Exercise 9–17: Devise a different definition for `set-cons` that maintains sets in some sorted order, making the test for set membership, and hence `set-cons` itself, potentially more efficient.

9-5 Defining Abstract Objects

This example demonstrates a syntactic extension that facilitates the definition of simple abstract objects (see Section 2–9). This facility has unlimited potential as the basis for a complete object-oriented subsystem in Scheme.

Abstract objects are similar to structures. However, rather than simply allowing field access and assignment as for structures, abstract objects respond to *messages*. The valid messages and the actions to be taken for each message are defined by code within the object itself rather than by code outside of the object, resulting in more modular and potentially more secure programming systems. The data local to an abstract object is accessible only through the actions performed by the object in response to the messages.

A particular type of abstract object is defined with `define-object`, which has a syntax similar to `define-structure` (Section 8–2). The general form is

```
(define-object (name id1 ...)
  ([id2 val] ...)
  ([msg action] ...))
```

where the first set of bindings ([*id2 val*] ...) may be omitted. `define-object` defines a procedure that is called to create new abstract objects of the given type. This procedure is called make-*name*, and the arguments to this procedure become the values of the local identifiers *id1* .... After the procedure is invoked, the identifiers *id2* ... are bound to the values *val* ... in sequence (as with `let*`) and the messages *msg* are bound to the procedure values *action* ... in a mutually recursive fashion (as with `letrec`). Within these bindings, the new abstract object is created; this object is the value of the creation procedure.

The syntactic form **send-message** is used to send messages to abstract objects. (**send-message** *object msg arg* ...) sends *object* the message *msg* with arguments *arg* .... When an object receives a message, the *arg* ... become the parameters to the action procedure associated with the message, and the value returned by this procedure is returned by **send-message**.

The following examples should help to clarify how abstract objects are defined and used. The first example is a simple **kons** object that is similar to Scheme's built-in pair object type, except that to access or assign its fields requires sending it messsages.

```
(define-object (kons kar kdr)
  ([get-car (lambda () kar)]
   [get-cdr (lambda () kdr)]
   [set-car! (lambda (x) (set! kar x))]
   [set-cdr! (lambda (x) (set! kdr x))]))
```

```
(define p (kons 'a 'b))
(send-message p get-car)        ⇒ a
(send-message p get-cdr)        ⇒ b
(send-message p set-cdr! 'c)
(send-message p get-cdr)        ⇒ c
```

The simple **kons** object does nothing but return or assign one of the fields as requested; this sort of object can be defined with **define-structure**, as we have seen. What makes abstract objects interesting is that they can be used to restrict access or perform additional services. The following version of **kons** requires that a password be given with any request to assign one of the fields. This password is a parameter to the **kons** procedure.

```
(define-object (kons kar kdr pwd)
  ([get-car (lambda () kar)]
   [get-cdr (lambda () kar)]
   [set-car!
     (lambda (x p)
       (when (string=? p pwd)
         (set! kar x)))]
   [set-cdr!
     (lambda (x p)
       (when (string=? p pwd)
```

```
                    (set! kar x)))])))

    (define p1 (kons 'a 'b "magnificent"))
    (send-message p1 set-car! 'c "magnificent")
    (send-message p1 get-car)                      ⇒ c
    (send-message p1 set-car! 'd "please")
    (send-message p1 get-car)                      ⇒ c
    (define p2 (kons 'x 'y "please"))
    (send-message p2 set-car! 'z "please")
    (send-message p2 get-car)                      ⇒ z
```

One important ability of an abstract object is that it can keep statistics on messages sent to it. The following version of kons counts accesses to the two fields. This version also demonstrates the use of explicitly initialized local bindings.

```
    (define-object (kons kar kdr)
      ([count 0])
      ([get-car
        (lambda ()
           (set! count (+ count 1))
           kar)]
       [get-cdr
        (lambda ()
           (set! count (+ count 1))
           kdr)]
       [accesses
        (lambda () count)]))

    (define p (kons 'a 'b))
    (send-message p get-car)   ⇒ a
    (send-message p get-cdr)   ⇒ b
    (send-message p accesses)  ⇒ 2
    (send-message p get-cdr)   ⇒ b
    (send-message p accesses)  ⇒ 3
```

The implementation of define-object is straightforward. The object definition is transformed into a definition of the object creation procedure. This procedure is the value of a lambda expression whose arguments are those specified in the definition. The body of the lambda consists of a let* expression to bind the local identifiers, and a letrec expression to bind the message names to the action procedures. The body of the letrec is another lambda expression whose value represents the new object. The body of this lambda expression compares the messages passed in with the expected messages using a case expression and applies the corresponding action procedure to the remaining arguments.

For example, the definition

```
(define-object (kons kar kdr)
  ([count 0])
  ([get-car
    (lambda ()
      (set! count (+ count 1))
      kar)]
   [get-cdr
    (lambda ()
      (set! count (+ count 1))
      kdr)]
   [accesses
    (lambda () count)]))
```

is transformed into

```
(define kons
  (lambda (kar kdr)
    (let* ([count 0])
      (letrec ([get-car
                (lambda ()
                  (set! count (+ count 1)) kar)]
               [get-cdr
                (lambda ()
                  (set! count (+ count 1)) kdr)]
               [accesses (lambda () count)])
        (lambda (msg . args)
          (case msg
            [get-car (apply get-car args)]
            [get-cdr (apply get-cdr args)]
            [accesses (apply accesses args)]
            [else
             (error 'kons "invalid message ~s"
                    (cons msg args))]))))))
```

Here is the code.

```
;;; define-object creates an object, using let* to bind the local
;;; fields and letrec to define the exported procedures. An object
;;; is itself a procedure that accepts messages corresponding to the
;;; names of the exported procedures. The second pattern is used to
;;; allow the set of local fields to be omitted.
(extend-syntax (define-object)
  [(define-object (name . idlist)
      ([id1 val1] ...)
      ([id2 val2] ...))
    (define name
      (lambda idlist
        (let* ([id1 val1] ...)
          (letrec ([id2 val2] ...)
            (lambda (msg . args)
              (case msg
                [id2 (apply id2 args)] ...
                [else
                  (error 'name "invalid message ~s"
                    (cons msg args))]))))))]
  [(define-object (name . idlist)
      ([id2 val2] ...))
    (define-object (name . idlist)
      ()
      ([id2 val2] ...))])
;;; send-message abstracts the act of sending a message from the act
;;; of applying a procedure, and allows the message to be unquoted.
(extend-syntax (send-message)
  [(send-message obj msg arg ...)
    (obj 'msg arg ...)])
```

Exercise 9–18: Use define-object to define the stack object type from Section 2–9.

Exercise 9–19: Use define-object to define a queue object type. A queue object should accept the messages empty?, get! (removes and returns the first element), and put! (adds an element to the end of the queue). Elements should be removed in the same order they are entered.

Exercise 9–20: It is often useful to describe one object in terms of another. For example, the second kons object type could be described as the same as the first but with a password argument and different actions associated with the set-car! and set-cdr! messages. This is called *inheritance*; the new type of object is said to *inherit* attributes from the first. Modify define-object to support inheritance by allowing the optional declaration (inherit object-name) to appear after the message/action pairs. This will require saving some information about each object definition for possible use in subsequent object definitions. Conflicting argument names should be disallowed, but other conflicts should be resolved by using the initialization or action specified in the new object definition.

Exercise 9–21: What if we want to describe an object type in terms of not just one but of two or more existing object types? Further modify define-object to support *multiple inheritance* by extending the inherit expression to allow multiple object names. What should happen if two or more inherited objects initialize a conflicting identifier or message name differently?

9-6 A Unification Algorithm

Unification [16] is a pattern-matching technique used in automated theorem proving, type-inference systems, computer algebra, and logic programming, *e.g.*, Prolog [2].

A unification algorithm attempts to make two symbolic expressions equal by computing a unifying substitution for the expressions. A *substitution* is a function that replaces variables with other expressions. A substitution must treat all occurrences of a variable the same way, *e.g.*, if it replaces one occurrence of the variable x by a, it must replace all occurrences of x by a. A unifying substitution, or *unifier*, for two expressions e_1 and e_2 is a substitution, σ, such that $\sigma(e_1) = \sigma(e_2)$.

For example, the two expressions $f(x)$ and $f(y)$ can be unified by substituting x for y (or y for x). In this case, the unifier σ could be described as the function that replaces y with x and leaves other variables unchanged. On the other hand, the two expressions $x + 1$ and $y + 2$ cannot be unified. It might appear that substituting 3 for x and 2 for y would make both expressions equal to 4, and hence equal to each other. However, the symbolic expressions themselves, $3 + 1$ and $2 + 2$, still differ.

Two expressions may have more than one unifier. For example, the expressions $f(x, y)$ and $f(1, y)$ can be unified to $f(1, y)$ with the substitution of 1 for x. They may also be unified to $f(1, 5)$ with the substitution of 1 for x and 5 for y. The first substitution is preferable, since it does not commit us to the unnecessary replacement of y. Unification algorithms typically produce the *most general unifier*, or *mgu*, for two expressions. The mgu for two expressions makes no unnecessary substitutions; all other unifiers for the expressions are special cases of the mgu. In the example above, the first substitution is the mgu and the second is a special case.

For the purposes of this program, a symbolic expression can be a variable, a constant, or a function application. Variables are represented by Scheme symbols, *e.g.*, x; a function application is represented by a list with the function name in the first position and its arguments in the remaining positions, *e.g.*, (f x); and constants are represented by zero-arity functions, *e.g.*, (a).

The algorithm presented here finds the mgu for two terms, if it exists, using a *continuation-passing style*, or *CPS*, approach to recursion on subterms. Continuation passing style uses ordinary procedures (not the continuation objects created by call/cc) as explicit *success* and *failure* continuations. A procedure passed an explicit continuation procedure does not usually return directly to its caller. Instead, it either passes the continuation on in a tail call, or it invokes the continuation explicitly in a tail call. Using explicit success or failure continuations or both can sometimes help to avoid the extra communication necessary to separate successful execution of a procedure from unsuccessful execution. Also, though it is not shown here, continuation passing style allows a procedure to pass more than one result back to its caller, because the procedure which implements the continuation can take any number of arguments. Furthermore, it is possible to have multiple success or failure continuations for different flavors of success or failure, each possibly taking different numbers and types of arguments.

The procedure unify takes two terms and passes them to a help procedure, uni, along with an initial (identity) substitution, a success continuation, and a failure continuation. The success continuation returns the result of applying its argument, a substitution, to one of the terms, *i.e.*, the unified result. The failure continuation simply returns its argument, a message. Because control passes by explicit continuation within unify (always with tail calls), a return from the success or failure continuation is a return from unify itself.

Substitutions are procedures. Whenever a variable is to be replaced by another term, a new substitution is formed from the variable, the term, and the existing substitution. Given a term as an argument, the new substitution replaces occurrences of its saved identifier with its saved term in the result of invoking the saved substitution on the argument expression. Intuitively, a substitution is a chain of procedures, one for each variable in the substitution. The chain is terminated by the initial, identity substitution.

Here are some simple examples demonstrating unify.

```
(unify 'x 'y)                          ⇒ y
(unify '(f x y) '(g x y))              ⇒ "clash"
(unify '(f x (h)) '(f (h) y))          ⇒ (f (h) (h))
(unify '(f (g x) y) '(f y x))          ⇒ "loop"
(unify '(f (g x) y) '(f y (g x)))      ⇒ (f (g x) (g x))
```

Here is the code.

```
;;; unify is given its value in the body of the letrec
(define unify #f)
(letrec
    ;; occurs? returns #t iff u occurs in v
    ([occurs?
        (lambda (u v)
            (and (pair? v)
                 (let f ([l (cdr v)])
                     (and l
                         (or (eq? u (car l))
                             (occurs? u (car l))
                             (f (cdr l)))))))]
    ;; sigma returns a new substitution procedure extending s by
    ;; the substitution of u with v
    [sigma
        (lambda (u v s)
            (lambda (x)
                (let f ([x (s x)])
                    (if (symbol? x)
                        (if (eq? x u) v x)
                        (cons (car x) (map f (cdr x)))))))]
    ;; try-subst tries to substitute u for v, but may require a
    ;; full unification if (s u) is not a variable, and it may
    ;; fail if it sees that u occurs in v.
```

```
[try-subst
   (lambda (u v s ks kf)
      (let ([u (s u)])
         (if (not (symbol? u))
             (uni u v s ks kf)
             (let ([v (s v)])
                (cond
                   [(eq? u v) (ks s)]
                   [(occurs? u v) (kf "loop")]
                   [else (ks (sigma u v s))]))))))]
```

;; uni attempts to unify u and v with a continuation-passing
;; style that returns a substitution to the success argument
;; ks or an error message to the failure argument kf. The
;; substitution itself is represented by a procedure from
;; variables to terms.

```
[uni
   (lambda (u v s ks kf)
      (cond
         [(symbol? u) (try-subst u v s ks kf)]
         [(symbol? v) (try-subst v u s ks kf)]
         [(and (eq? (car u) (car v))
               (= (length u) (length v)))
          (let f ([u (cdr u)] [v (cdr v)] [s s])
             (if (null? u)
                 (ks s)
                 (uni (car u)
                      (car v)
                      s
                      (lambda (s) (f (cdr u) (cdr v) s))
                      kf)))]
         [else (kf "clash")])))]
```

;; unify shows one possible interface to uni, where the initial
;; substitution is the identity procedure, the initial success
;; continuation returns the unified term and the initial failure
;; continuation returns the error message.

```
(set! unify
   (lambda (u v)
      (uni u
           v
```

```
(lambda (x) x)
(lambda (s) (s u))
(lambda (msg) msg)))))
```

Exercise 9–22: Modify unify so that it returns its substitution rather than printing the unified term. Apply this substitution to both input terms to verify that it returns the same result for each.

Exercise 9–23: As is mentioned above, substitutions on a term are performed sequentially, requiring one entire pass through the input expression for each substituted variable. Represent the substitution differently so that only one pass through the expression need be made. Make sure that substitutions are performed not only on the input expression but also on any expressions you insert during substitution.

Exercise 9–24: Extend the continuation-passing style unification algorithm into an entire continuation-passing style logic programming system.

9-7 Engines from Continuations

This implementation of engines with continuations and timers demonstrates the use of continuations, timer interrupts, and the exception handling system in general. Engines are introduced in Section 4–7.

The engine code defines three procedures: make-engine, engine-block, and engine-return. Keyboard interrupts, stack interrupts, and errors are caught while an engine is running so that the engine may be disabled before the appropriate handler is invoked.

All of the code is defined within the scope of five identifiers that hold the state of the engine system:

active?, true if and only if an engine is running,

escape, the continuation to the engine invoker,

saved-error, the saved error handler,

saved-keybd, the saved keyboard-interrupt handler, and

saved-stack, the saved stack-overflow handler.

Whenever active? is false, the values of the remaining identifiers are unimportant.

One important rule governing this code is that nothing is ever done with the timer running. The reason is that an errant timer interrupt could occur with the code in an unknown state. There are four logically separate entries into the code with the timer running: run-engine when the user attempts to invoke a nested engine, block when the user explicitly calls the engine-block procedure, return when the expression terminates or the user explicitly invokes engine-return, and any of the handlers created by exception when an error or interrupt occurs. Each of these entries immediately disables the timer by evaluating (set-timer 0).

The identifier active? is used to detect attempts to nest engines in order to prevent corruption of the engine system and to provide an error message for the user. It is also used to protect against attempts to invoke engine-block or engine-return while no engine is active.

The identifier escape holds the continuation of the most recent invocation of run-engine from within the engine procedure (see the definition of engine in the code below). This continuation is invoked by block with a thunk; this thunk encapsulates the continuation of the interrupted computation. The continuation may also be invoked by return with a pair holding the value of the computation and the number of ticks remaining. When the continuation is invoked, control returns to the procedure created by engine, and this procedure invokes the caller's expire or complete argument depending on the type of object it receives (procedure or pair).

An engine expression that completes automatically returns to the invoker of the engine because of the return waiting for the value of the thunk in run-engine. But notice what happens in block. block returns a thunk that is made into an engine before being passed as the argument to expire. When this engine is later invoked by run-engine the thunk ignores the continuation of its invocation, specifically the call to return, by immediately invoking the continuation of the interrupted program. Although this may seem incorrect, it works out fine because the continuation of the interrupted program has a pending call to return from when it was first started.

Here is the code.

```
;;; engine-return, engine-block, and make-engine are given values
;;; inside the body of the letrec below.
(define engine-return #f)
(define engine-block #f)
(define make-engine #f)
(letrec
    ;; active? is true when an engine is running.
    ([active? #f]
     ;; escape holds the continuation to the engine invoker
```

```
[escape #f]
;; saved-error holds the saved error handler
[saved-error #f]
;; saved-keybd holds the saved keyboard-interrupt handler
[saved-keybd #f]
;; saved-stack holds the saved stack-overflow handler
[saved-stack #f]
;; clean up the state, return time left
[sanitize
   (lambda ()
      (set! active? #f)
      (set! *error-handler* saved-error)
      (set! *keyboard-interrupt-handler* saved-keybd)
      (set! *stack-overflow-handler* saved-stack))]
;; disable engine and return the continuation
[block
   (lambda ()
      (set-timer 0)
      (unless active?
         (error 'engine-block "no engine active"))
      (sanitize)
      (call/cc
         (lambda (c)
            (escape (lambda () (c #f))))))]
;; disable engine and return pair (value . ticks)
[return
   (lambda (x)
      (let ([n (set-timer 0)])
         (unless active?
            (error 'engine-return "no engine active"))
         (sanitize)
         (escape (cons x n))))]
;; disable engine and call the handler
[exception
   (lambda (handler)
      (lambda args
         (set-timer 0)
         (sanitize)
         (apply handler args)
```

```
                    ; in case the handler returns
                    (error 'engine "engine aborted")))]
;; new handlers for stack, keyboard, error
[setup-handlers
   (lambda ()
      (set! saved-error *error-handler*)
      (set! *error-handler*
            (exception saved-error))
      (set! saved-keybd *keyboard-interrupt-handler*)
      (set! *keyboard-interrupt-handler*
            (exception saved-keybd))
      (set! saved-stack *stack-overflow-handler*)
      (set! *stack-overflow-handler*
            (exception saved-stack)))]
;; run a thunk as an engine
[run-engine
   (lambda (thunk ticks)
      (call/cc
         (lambda (k)
            ; check for nested engines
            (set-timer 0)
            (when active?
               (error 'engine "cannot nest engines"))
            ; start your engines
            (setup-handlers)
            (set! escape k)
            (set! active? #t)
            (set! *timer-interrupt-handler* block)
            (set-timer ticks)
            ; go!
            (return (thunk)))))]
;; create an engine from a thunk
[engine
   (lambda (thunk)
      (lambda (ticks complete expire)
         (let ([x (run-engine thunk ticks)])
            ; x is a thunk (block) or pair (return)
            (if (procedure? x)
                (expire (engine x))
```

```
                    (complete (car x) (cdr x)))))))])
;; establish top-level values for engine-return, engine-block and
;; make-engine
(set! engine-return return)
(set! engine-block block)
(set! make-engine engine))
```

Exercise 9–25: This code may appear to be correct, but an untimely keyboard or stack interrupt could corrupt the engine system. Use `critical-section` where necessary to avoid this possible problem.

Exercise 9–26: This implementation of engines does not allow one engine to call another, *i.e.*, nested engines. Modify the implementation to allow nested engines.

Exercise 9–27: Implement the kernel of a small operating system using engines for processes. Processes should request services (such as reading input from the user) by evaluating an expression of the form `(trap 'request)`. Use `engine-return` to implement `trap`. Why is `engine-block` not appropriate?

Exercise 9–28: Write the same operating-system kernel without using engines, building instead from continuations and timer interrupts.

References

[1] Harold Abelson and Gerald J. Sussman with Julie Sussman, *Structure and Interpretation of Computer Programs*, MIT Press, 1985.

[2] William F. Clocksin and Christopher S. Mellish, *Programming in Prolog*, 2d. ed., Springer-Verlag, 1984.

[3] Daniel P. Friedman, Christopher T. Haynes, and Eugene E. Kohlbecker, "Programming with Continuations," in *Program Transformation and Programming Environments*, ed. P. Pepper, Springer-Verlag, 1984, 263–274.

[4] Daniel P. Friedman and Matthias Felleisen, *The Little LISPer*, MIT Press, 1987; Science Research Associates, 1986.

[5] Christopher T. Haynes, Daniel P. Friedman, and Mitchell Wand, "Obtaining Coroutines with Continuations," *Journal of Computer Languages* *11*, 3/4, 1986, 143–153.

[6] Christopher T. Haynes and Daniel P. Friedman, "Abstracting Timed Preemption with Engines," *Journal of Computer Languages*, to appear.

[7] Christopher T. Haynes and Daniel P. Friedman, "Embedding Continuations in Procedural Objects," *Transactions on Programming Languages and Systems*, to appear.

[8] Kathleen Jensen and Niklaus Wirth, *Pascal User Manual and Report*, 2d. ed., Springer-Verlag, 1974.

[9] Brian W. Kernighan and Dennis M. Ritchie, *The C Programming Language*, Prentice-Hall, 1978.

[10] Donald E. Knuth, *The Art of Computer Programming*, Vol I: *Fundamental Algorithms*, 2d. ed., Addison Wesley, 1985, 78–79.

[11] Eugene E. Kohlbecker, *Syntactic Extensions in the Programming Language Lisp*, Ph.D. Thesis, Indiana University, 1986.

[12] Elliott Mendelson, *Introduction to Mathematical Logic*, D. Van Nostrand Company, Inc., 1984, 102–104.

[13] Peter Naur, et al., "Revised Report on the Algorithmic Language ALGOL 60," *Communications of the ACM 6*, 1, January 1963, 1–17.

[14] David A. Plaisted, "Constructs for Sets, Quantifiers, and Rewrite Rules in Lisp," University of Illinois at Urbana-Champaign Department of Computer Science Report UIUCDCS-R-84-1176, June 1984.

[15] Jonathan A. Rees and William Clinger, eds., "The Revised[3] Report on the Algorithmic Language Scheme," *Sigplan Notices 21*, 12, December 1986.

[16] J. A. Robinson, "A Machine-Oriented Logic based on the Resolution Principle," *Journal of the ACM 12*, 1, 1965, 23–41.

[17] Guy L. Steele, Jr. and Gerald J. Sussman, "The Revised Report on Scheme, a Dialect of Lisp," MIT Artificial Intelligence Memo 452, January 1978.

[18] Guy L. Steele, Jr., *Common LISP: The Language*, Digital Press, 1984.

[19] Gerald J. Sussman and Guy L. Steele, Jr., "Scheme: an Interpreter for Extended Lambda Calculus," MIT Artificial Intelligence Memo 349, December 1975.

[20] Mitchell Wand, "Continuation-Based Multiprocessing," *Conference Record of the 1980 LISP Conference*, August 1980, 19–28.

Summary of Forms

The table which follows summarizes the Scheme syntactic forms and procedures described in Chapters 3 through 8. It shows the category of the form and the section number where it is defined. The category states whether the form describes a syntactic form or a procedure; it also states whether the form is an essential or optional feature according to the "Revised[3] Report on the Algorithmic Language Scheme." The abbreviations used to describe the category are as follows:

- *ess. proc.* or *ess. syn.* an essential procedure or syntactic form (described in the Revised[3] Report and required of all Scheme implementations).
- *opt. proc.* or *opt. syn.* an optional procedure or syntactic form (described in the Revised[3] Report but not required of all Scheme implementations).
- *ext. proc.* or *ext. syn.* an extended procedure or syntactic form (not described in the Revised[3] Report).

Form	Category		Sect
(* num_1 num_2)	ess.	proc.	5–3
(* num ...)	opt.	proc.	5–3
(+ num_1 num_2)	ess.	proc.	5–3
(+ num ...)	opt.	proc.	5–3
(- num_1 num_2)	ess.	proc.	5–3
(- num_1 num_2 ...)	opt.	proc.	5–3
(/ num_1 num_2)	ess.	proc.	5–3
(/ num_1 num_2 ...)	opt.	proc.	5–3
(1+ num)	ext.	proc.	5–3
(1- num)	ext.	proc.	5–3
(< $real_1$ $real_2$)	ess.	proc.	5–3
(< $real_1$ $real_2$ ...)	opt.	proc.	5–3
(<= $real_1$ $real_2$)	ess.	proc.	5–3
(<= $real_1$ $real_2$ ...)	opt.	proc.	5–3
(= num_1 num_2)	ess.	proc.	5–3
(= num_1 num_2 ...)	opt.	proc.	5–3
(> $real_1$ $real_2$)	ess.	proc.	5–3
(> $real_1$ $real_2$ ...)	opt.	proc.	5–3
(>= $real_1$ $real_2$)	ess.	proc.	5–3
(>= $real_1$ $real_2$ ...)	opt.	proc.	5–3
(abort)	ext.	proc.	7–3

(cdadar *pair*)	ess.	proc.	5-2
(cdaddr *pair*)	ess.	proc.	5-2
(cdadr *pair*)	ess.	proc.	5-2
(cdar *pair*)	ess.	proc.	5-2
(cddaar *pair*)	ess.	proc.	5-2
(cddadr *pair*)	ess.	proc.	5-2
(cddar *pair*)	ess.	proc.	5-2
(cdddar *pair*)	ess.	proc.	5-2
(cddddr *pair*)	ess.	proc.	5-2
(cddddr *pair*)	ess.	proc.	5-2
(cdddr *pair*)	ess.	proc.	5-2
(cddr *pair*)	ess.	proc.	5-2
(cdr *pair*)	ess.	proc.	5-2
(ceiling *real*)	opt.	proc.	5-3
(char->integer *char*)	ess.	proc.	5-4
(char-alphabetic? *char*)	opt.	proc.	5-4
(char-ci<=? *char$_1$ char$_2$ ...*)	opt.	proc.	5-4
(char-ci<? *char$_1$ char$_2$ ...*)	opt.	proc.	5-4
(char-ci=? *char$_1$ char$_2$ ...*)	opt.	proc.	5-4
(char-ci>=? *char$_1$ char$_2$ ...*)	opt.	proc.	5-4
(char-ci>? *char$_1$ char$_2$ ...*)	opt.	proc.	5-4
(char-downcase *char*)	opt.	proc.	5-4
(char-lower-case? *letter*)	opt.	proc.	5-4
(char-numeric? *char*)	opt.	proc.	5-4
(char-ready?)	opt.	proc.	6-1
(char-ready? *input-port*)	opt.	proc.	6-1
(char-upcase *char*)	opt.	proc.	5-4
(char-upper-case? *letter*)	opt.	proc.	5-4
(char-whitespace? *char*)	opt.	proc.	5-4
(char<=? *char$_1$ char$_2$*)	ess.	proc.	5-4
(char<=? *char$_1$ char$_2$ ...*)	opt.	proc.	5-4
(char<? *char$_1$ char$_2$*)	ess.	proc.	5-4
(char<? *char$_1$ char$_2$ ...*)	opt.	proc.	5-4
(char=? *char$_1$ char$_2$*)	ess.	proc.	5-4
(char=? *char$_1$ char$_2$ ...*)	opt.	proc.	5-4
(char>=? *char$_1$ char$_2$*)	ess.	proc.	5-4
(char>=? *char$_1$ char$_2$ ...*)	opt.	proc.	5-4
(char>? *char$_1$ char$_2$*)	ess.	proc.	5-4
(char>? *char$_1$ char$_2$ ...*)	opt.	proc.	5-4
(char? *obj*)	ess.	proc.	5-1
(clear-input-port)	ext.	proc.	6-1
(clear-input-port *input-port*)	ext.	proc.	6-1
(clear-output-port)	ext.	proc.	6-2
(clear-output-port *output-port*)	ext.	proc.	6-2
(close-input-port *input-port*)	opt.	proc.	6-1
(close-output-port *output-port*)	opt.	proc.	6-2

(extend-syntax (*name key* ...) (*pattern fender expansion*) ...)	ext.	syn.	8–1
(floor *real*)	opt.	proc.	5–3
(fluid-let ((*id val*) ...) *exp₁ exp₂* ...)	ext.	syn.	3–5
(flush-output-port)	ext.	proc.	6–2
(flush-output-port *output-port*)	ext.	proc.	6–2
(for-each *procedure list*)	ess.	proc.	4–5
(for-each *procedure list₁ list₂* ...)	opt.	proc.	4–5
(force *promise*)	opt.	proc.	4–8
(format *format-string obj* ...)	ext.	proc.	6–3
(fprintf *output-port format-string obj* ...)	ext.	proc.	6–3
(gcd *int* ...)	opt.	proc.	5–3
(gensym)	ext.	proc.	5–7
(get-output-string *string-output-port*)	ext.	proc.	6–2
(getprop *symbol key*)	ext.	proc.	5–7
(if *test-exp then-exp else-exp*)	ess.	syn.	4–4
(if *test-exp then-exp*)	opt.	syn.	4–4
(imag-part *num*)	opt.	proc.	5–3
(inexact->exact *num*)	opt.	proc.	5–3
(inexact? *num*)	ess.	proc.	5–3
(input-port? *obj*)	ess.	proc.	5–1
(integer->char *int*)	ess.	proc.	5–4
(integer? *obj*)	ess.	proc.	5–1
(*keyboard-interrupt-handler*)	ext.	proc.	7–9
(lambda *idspec exp₁ exp₂* ...)	ess.	syn.	3–1
(last-pair *list*)	opt.	proc.	5–2
(lcm *int* ...)	opt.	proc.	5–3
(length *list*)	ess.	proc.	5–2
(let ((*id val*) ...) *exp₁ exp₂* ...)	ess.	syn.	3–2
(let *name* ((*id val*) ...) *exp₁ exp₂* ...)	opt.	syn.	4–5
(let* ((*id val*) ...) *exp₁ exp₂* ...)	opt.	syn.	3–2
(letrec ((*id val*) ...) *exp₁ exp₂* ...)	ess.	syn.	3–2
(list *obj* ...)	ess.	proc.	5–2
(list* *obj* ... *final-obj*)	ext.	proc.	5–2
(list->string *list*)	ess.	proc.	5–5
(list->vector *list*)	ess.	proc.	5–6
(list-copy *list*)	ext.	proc.	5–2
(list-ref *list n*)	opt.	proc.	5–2
(list-tail *list n*)	opt.	proc.	5–2
(list? *obj*)	ext.	proc.	5–1
(load *filename*)	ess.	proc.	7–1
(load *filename eval-proc*)	ext.	proc.	7–1
(log *num*)	opt.	proc.	5–3
(magnitude *num*)	opt.	proc.	5–3
(make-engine *thunk*)	ext.	proc.	4–7
(make-list *n*)	ext.	proc.	5–2
(make-list *n obj*)	ext.	proc.	5–2

(make-polar $real_1$ $real_2$)	opt.	proc.	5–3
(make-rectangular $real_1$ $real_2$)	opt.	proc.	5–3
(make-string int)	opt.	proc.	5–5
(make-string int $char$)	opt.	proc.	5–5
(make-vector n)	ess.	proc.	5–6
(make-vector n obj)	opt.	proc.	5–6
(map $procedure$ $list$)	ess.	proc.	4–5
(map $procedure$ $list_1$ $list_2$ ...)	opt.	proc.	4–5
(max $real_1$ $real_2$)	ess.	proc.	5–3
(max $real_1$ $real_2$ ...)	opt.	proc.	5–3
(member obj $list$)	ess.	proc.	5–2
(memq obj $list$)	ess.	proc.	5–2
(memv obj $list$)	ess.	proc.	5–2
(merge $predicate$ $list_1$ $list_2$)	ext.	proc.	5–2
(merge! $predicate$ $list_1$ $list_2$)	ext.	proc.	5–2
(min $real_1$ $real_2$)	ess.	proc.	5–3
(min $real_1$ $real_2$ ...)	opt.	proc.	5–3
(modulo int_1 int_2)	opt.	proc.	5–3
(negative? num)	ess.	proc.	5–3
(new-cafe)	ext.	proc.	7–3
(newline)	ess.	proc.	6–2
(newline $output$-$port$)	ess.	proc.	6–2
(not obj)	ess.	proc.	4–4
(null? obj)	ess.	proc.	5–1
(number? obj)	ess.	proc.	5–1
(numerator rat)	opt.	proc.	5–3
(odd? int)	ess.	proc.	5–3
(open-input-file $filename$)	opt.	proc.	6–1
(open-input-string $string$)	ext.	proc.	6–1
(open-output-file $filename$)	opt.	proc.	6–2
(open-output-string)	ext.	proc.	6–2
(or exp ...)	opt.	syn.	4–4
(ormap $procedure$ $list_1$ $list_2$ ...)	ext.	proc.	4–5
(output-port? obj)	ess.	proc.	5–1
(pair? obj)	ess.	proc.	5–1
(positive? $real$)	ess.	proc.	5–3
(pretty-print obj)	ext.	proc.	6–2
(pretty-print obj $output$-$port$)	ext.	proc.	6–2
(printf $format$-$string$ obj ...)	ext.	proc.	6–3
($procedure$ exp ...)	ess.	syn.	4–1
(procedure? obj)	ess.	proc.	5–1
(putprop $symbol$ key $value$)	ext.	proc.	5–7
(quasiquote obj)	opt.	syn.	4–2
(quote obj)	ess.	syn.	4–2
(quotient int_1 int_2)	ess.	proc.	5–3
(random int)	ext.	proc.	5–3

`(rational? obj)`	ess.	proc.	5–1
`(rationalize real`$_1$`)`	opt.	proc.	5–3
`(rationalize real`$_1$` real`$_2$`)`	opt.	proc.	5–3
`(read)`	ess.	proc.	6–1
`(read input-port)`	ess.	proc.	6–1
`(read-char)`	ess.	proc.	6–1
`(read-char input-port)`	ess.	proc.	6–1
`(real-part num)`	opt.	proc.	5–3
`(real-time)`	ext.	proc.	7–6
`(real? obj)`	ess.	proc.	5–1
`(rec id exp)`	ext.	syn.	3–2
`(record-case val (key idspec exp ...) ... (else exp ...))`	ext.	syn.	4–4
`(record-case val (key idspec exp ...) ...)`	ext.	syn.	4–4
`(remainder int`$_1$` int`$_2$`)`	ess.	proc.	5–3
`(remove obj list)`	ext.	proc.	5–2
`(remove! obj list)`	ext.	proc.	5–2
`(remq obj list)`	ext.	proc.	5–2
`(remq! obj list)`	ext.	proc.	5–2
`(remv obj list)`	ext.	proc.	5–2
`(remv! obj list)`	ext.	proc.	5–2
`(reset)`	ext.	proc.	7–3
`(reverse list)`	opt.	proc.	5–2
`(reverse! list)`	ext.	proc.	5–2
`(round real)`	opt.	proc.	5–3
`(set! id exp)`	ess.	syn.	3–4
`(set-box! box obj)`	ext.	proc.	5–8
`(set-car! pair obj)`	ess.	proc.	5–2
`(set-cdr! pair obj)`	ess.	proc.	5–2
`(set-timer ticks)`	ext.	proc.	7–9
`(set-top-level-value! symbol obj)`	ext.	proc.	7–2
`(sin num)`	opt.	proc.	5–3
`(sort predicate list)`	ext.	proc.	5–2
`(sort! predicate list)`	ext.	proc.	5–2
`(sqrt num)`	opt.	proc.	5–3
`(*stack-overflow-handler*)`	ext.	proc.	7–9
`(string char ...)`	ext.	proc.	5–5
`(string->list string)`	ess.	proc.	5–5
`(string->symbol string)`	ess.	proc.	5–7
`(string->uninterned-symbol string)`	ext.	proc.	5–7
`(string-append string`$_1$` string`$_2$`)`	ess.	proc.	5–5
`(string-append string ...)`	opt.	proc.	5–5
`(string-ci<=? string`$_1$` string`$_2$` ...)`	opt.	proc.	5–5
`(string-ci<? string`$_1$` string`$_2$` ...)`	opt.	proc.	5–5
`(string-ci=? string`$_1$` string`$_2$` ...)`	opt.	proc.	5–5
`(string-ci>=? string`$_1$` string`$_2$` ...)`	opt.	proc.	5–5
`(string-ci>? string`$_1$` string`$_2$` ...)`	opt.	proc.	5–5

(vector *obj* ...)	ess.	proc.	5–6
(vector->list *vector*)	ess.	proc.	5–6
(vector-copy *vector*)	ext.	proc.	5–6
(vector-fill! *vector obj*)	opt.	proc.	5–6
(vector-length *vector*)	ess.	proc.	5–6
(vector-ref *vector n*)	ess.	proc.	5–6
(vector-set! *vector n obj*)	ess.	proc.	5–6
(vector? *obj*)	ess.	proc.	5–1
(waiter)	ext.	proc.	7–3
(when *test-exp exp$_1$ exp$_2$* ...)	ext.	syn.	4–4
(with ((*pattern expression*) ...) *expansion*)	ext.	syn.	8–1
(write *obj*)	ess.	proc.	6–2
(write *obj output-port*)	ess.	proc.	6–2
(write-char *char*)	ess.	proc.	6–2
(write-char *char output-port*)	ess.	proc.	6–2
(zero? *num*)	ess.	proc.	5–3

Index

T